D0817368

HOLY SWEET!

Indulgent Recipes for Bigger, Better Desserts

PEABODY JOHANSON

Founder of Sweet ReciPEAs

PAGE STREET
PUBLISHING CO.

WITHDRAWN

Hillsboro Public Library
Hillsboro, OR
A member of Washington County
COOPERATIVE LIBRARY SERVICES

PAGE STREET
PUBLISHING CO.

Copyright © 2020 Peabody Johanson

First published in 2020 by
Page Street Publishing Co.
27 Congress Street, Suite 105
Salem, MA 01970
www.pagestreetpublishing.com

All rights reserved. No part of this book may be reproduced or used, in any form or by any means, electronic or mechanical, without prior permission in writing from the publisher.

Distributed by Macmillan, sales in Canada by The Canadian Manda Group.

24 23 22 21 20   1 2 3 4 5

ISBN-13: 978-1-64567-156-5
ISBN-10: 1-64567-156-9

33614082137133

Library of Congress Control Number: 2019957245

Cover and book design by Kylie Alexander for Page Street Publishing Co.
Photography by Peabody Johanson

Printed and bound in China

Page Street Publishing protects our planet by donating to nonprofits like The Trustees, which focuses on local land conservation.

Dedicated to my mom, the woman who taught me to love baking.
To my husband, Jason, who supports me in all I do. To my longtime
blog readers, who pushed me to put out a book. To my friends
and family, who put up with me for months on end saying,
"Sure it's good, but is it cookbook-worthy good?"

CONTENTS

INTRODUCTION

EVIL TREATS FROM A NICE PERSON

That's my blog's tagline.

It came about because many of my readers call me evil, but in a good way. Evil genius way. Nice person might be up for debate. The biggest compliment I get from readers who have met me in person is that I'm just like I am on the blog.

Innovative. Creative. Unique. Decadent. Delicious. Accessible. Those are the words my readers use to describe my recipes, when asked. I'm not the girl you come to for a plain pound cake recipe. I haven't done anything normal when it comes to baking for as long as I can remember. Heck, I stuck a Twix bar in my cake the second time I used my Easy-Bake Oven as a kid.

My mother tells me I didn't get it from her—the culinary creativity, that is. And she is right. My mom substitutes dried cranberries for raisins and thinks she's being wild and crazy. She often asks me how I come up with this stuff, and I reply that I don't know. Because I don't. It's just how my mind works.

When my publishers first talked to me about doing a book, they were a little concerned that with fifteen years of blogging under my belt, I wouldn't have any new ideas for a cookbook. In one day I had more than 400 recipe ideas. The hard part was narrowing it all down to just 60 recipes. But rest assured, they are the best 60 recipes.

The other hard part was putting them into categories. I didn't want a cake section, a cookies section and so on. All cookbooks have those. I wanted something just a little bit different.

Because nostalgia plays a huge role in what I bake, I've decided to divide the book up according to that. Almost every event in my life can be tied back to some form of food. Every great memory has some meal or treat that links me to it. Whether it's all the foods we eat on Thanksgiving, or that every Christmas Eve we have pizza. Or that every Groundhog Day I eat a sprinkle donut and Chinese food. I don't remember my junior prom, but I remember that they had bowls of Goldfish crackers out everywhere. I can't tell you what my friend's grandmother looks like, but I can describe in great detail the amazing chocolate cake she served and refused to give me the recipe for.

The recipes in this book were made to brighten your mood. Bake your day, if you will. They were made with ingredients that you can almost always find at the grocery store. No real fancy equipment. The recipes were tested not only by me but by your average home cooks, many with tiny kitchens just like mine.

I have many hopes for this cookbook.

I hope you read this cookbook like a real book, from cover to cover. That's how I read cookbooks. I hope you earmark pages. I hope you find it worthy of a spot on your overburdened cookbook shelves because I know what an honor that is. I hope it inspires you to bake and create and to make food for others and share the love. I hope this cookbook fuels your creativity. And of course, I hope you love this cookbook. So much so that you give it as gifts to the fellow bakers in your life.

Most of all, I hope it makes you happy. That's the only reason I wrote it. Well, that and so my mom could tell people I'm a cookbook author. Because even after fifteen years of blogging my mom still calls my blog the "food internet thingy."

So go through and mark which recipe you want to make first. Then go make it!

Happy baking!
Peabody

TIPS FOR MAKING MY RECIPES

The most important tip I can give you when making my recipes is to realize you can make them. While you may look at some and think they seem daunting because the recipes are long, let me assure you that you *can* make them.

Growing up, I used to watch Martin Yan on PBS. While I had no big desire to cook Chinese food at home, it was his enthusiasm that drew me in. Every show he would end by saying, "If Yan can cook, so can you," and I believed him. Well, if Peabody can bake, so can you!

I'm not one of those bloggers with a giant kitchen, though I would surely like one. In fact, the kitchen I have now is the smallest I have ever had—and that includes my studio apartment when I was first out of college. All 81 square feet (7.5 square meters) of the kitchen I have now overflows with mixers (I have more than one), measuring cups, bowls, rolling pins, Bundt pans and just about everything else a baker would need. Everything I baked for this book was made in that tiny kitchen. Every recipe in this book can be made by the average home baker.

SERVING SIZES

You will see that almost every recipe in here uses the word "about." That is because over my fifteen years of blogging I have learned that no one cuts the same. What one person thinks is 1 inch (2.5 cm) another person does not. What I think is two-thirds full is not what other people think is two-thirds full. And with that, serving sizes vary. Greatly.

So "about." That's what I'm going with.

TIMING

Just like serving sizes, all prep and cooking times are an approximate. Cooking and baking times can vary greatly based on what type of stovetop and oven you have, either gas or electric. They all cook slightly different. Same for prep times. For example, if you are using a stand mixer with the whisk attachment to whip cream, that will go faster than using a mixing bowl and electric beaters.

The quality and age of the ingredients you are using can affect the timing, too. Even the temperature and humidity in your kitchen can change things. So "about." I'm sticking with it.

MIXERS

The recipes will say to use a stand mixer. I realize that not everyone owns a stand mixer, so just know that any time it says "stand mixer" you can use a large bowl and an electric handheld mixer all the same.

If you are an avid baker, though, and do not own one, I suggest you ask for one for your birthday or save up. They really are helpful.

THERMOMETERS

I am a *huge* proponent of owning a noncontact digital laser infrared thermometer. You can usually pick one up for around $20. There are certainly more expensive ones, but for baking and candy making you really don't need a top-of-the-line one.

Once I switched to the infrared thermometer, candy making became so much easier. So much. Where I used to fail miserably, I was finally finding success. I also use it to make Swiss meringue buttercream, which is used quite a bit in this book, as it's my favorite frosting.

You can certainly use the old-fashioned candy thermometers, but I'm telling you the digital is a game changer.

INGREDIENTS

Almost every ingredient in this book can be found at your local grocery store, with a few exceptions. And those you will most likely be able to find online.

SUBSTITUTIONS

Nothing in this book is low calorie or low fat. It is not meant to be. If you try to use skim milk instead of cream, your recipe will not turn out. When a recipe calls for ingredients such as milk, sour cream, buttermilk and cream cheese, I mean full fat. Try to reduce the sugar? The recipe will not turn out. Sugar is not only for sweetness but for structure. Trust me, I took a lot of science classes.

So while I encourage you to play around with flavors, I discourage you from trying to make my recipes better for you. They were never intended for that.

INNER CHILD

RECIPES INSPIRED BY MY CHILDHOOD FAVORITES

Honestly, in retrospect, I could have written a whole cookbook on just this subject. I was definitely a snack cake and store-bought cookie kid. My poor mom made treats all the time from scratch, but I was a product of great Saturday morning cartoon advertising.

As a kid, I wasn't that big of a chocolate fan. In fact, the only two chocolate snacks I liked were Donettes and Ding Dongs, both because of the chocolate coating.

One summer when my cousins came to stay with us for a few weeks, my aunt had bought Ding Dongs and put them in the fridge (we all liked them chilled). One of my many bright ideas was to go and open up all the Ding Dongs, eat all the chocolate coating off each one, and then wrap them back up as if nothing had happened. Amazingly, everyone figured out what had happened and who had done it. Clearly, my ninja skills needed work.

I was quirky about how I ate my snack cakes and cookies as a kid. Still am. Twinkies? Have to be frozen. Chocolate Donettes have to be heated for exactly seventeen seconds in the microwave to the precise moment when the coating starts to melt slightly.

I could go on. . . .

My love for all these goodies is on display in this chapter. While most of the recipes are *inspired* by snack cakes and cookies, there are a few recipes that actually have the item in them. Take the Circus Animal Filled Donuts (page 12) for example. You have to include the cookies because you cannot replicate that flavor in any way. . . . I have tried many, many times over the years. Especially for when they dare try to stop making them.

I hope these recipes make you smile and remind you of the carefree days of playing hide-and-seek with the neighbors, not having to pay bills, running around barefoot and of course, eating preservative-filled snack cakes and cookies.

CIRCUS ANIMAL FILLED DONUTS

YIELD
Makes 16

Of all the store-bought cookies, Circus Animal Cookies are my favorite. I'm not sure if it's the fun pink and white cookies studded with sprinkles, the fact that you have to spend an hour figuring out what animal the shape is supposed to be or the very waxy yet addicting coating on the outside that no other food on the planet tastes like. Whatever it is . . . I love them. While I thought about making from-scratch donuts (if you want, the Cinnamon Donut Peach Shortcake recipe on page 101 includes a from-scratch donut recipe), it made no sense for this recipe since my childhood donuts were made from deep-fried canned biscuits. Then the donuts are stuffed with a Circus Animal Cookie filling. All topped with pink and white glaze and rainbow nonpareils to make them extra fun.

CIRCUS ANIMAL COOKIE BAVARIAN CREAM

1 cup (240 ml) cold water, divided

1 (2¼-tsp [7-g]) packet powdered unflavored gelatin

3 large eggs, separated

¼ cup (50 g) granulated sugar, divided

1 cup (240 ml) heavy cream

1 tsp vanilla extract

3 drops of pink food coloring

1½ cups (80 g) crushed Circus Animal Cookies

To make the Circus Animal Cookie Bavarian cream: Place ¼ cup (60 ml) of water in a small bowl and sprinkle the gelatin over it. Let it dissolve, about 3 minutes.

In a large saucepan, whisk together the egg yolks and ⅛ cup (25 g) of granulated sugar. Do not place it over the heat yet. Bring the remaining water to a boil in another small saucepan. When it starts to boil, remove it from the heat. Temper the yolk and sugar mixture by slowly adding the boiling water, whisking the whole time.

Fill a large heatproof bowl with ice. Then put the saucepan with the yolk and sugar mixture on the stovetop and add the dissolved gelatin. Heat over medium-low heat and simmer, stirring constantly, until the sauce coats the back of a spoon, about 3 to 5 minutes. Set the saucepan in the ice-filled bowl. This will help the mixture cool quicker. Watch to make sure the gelatin doesn't start to set. (If your gelatin starts to set, pour the mixture into the bowl of a stand mixer fitted with the whisk attachment and beat until it's smooth, about 3 minutes.) Once it's cool, remove the saucepan from the ice bath and set it aside.

In the bowl of a stand mixer with the whisk attachment, whip the cream into stiff peaks, about 7 to 8 minutes. Add the vanilla and whip until it's fully incorporated. Set aside.

In another bowl of a stand mixer with the whisk attachment, whip the egg whites and the remaining ⅛ cup (25 g) of granulated sugar until stiff peaks form, about 3 to 5 minutes. Carefully fold the egg whites into the whipped cream. Then fold the egg white and cream mixture into the cooled gelatin mixture. Add the food coloring and mix until the color is evenly dispersed. Fold in the Circus Animal Cookie pieces and mix until they're fully combined.

(continued)

CIRCUS ANIMAL FILLED DONUTS (CONTINUED)

Cover the mixture with plastic wrap and refrigerate at least 2 hours, until it has set. Then put it in a piping bag fitted with a plain tip (size 4).

To make the donuts: Heat the oil in a deep skillet until the temperature reaches 375°F (190°C). While the oil is heating, lay out a sheet of wax paper, separate the 16 biscuits and lay them out on the wax paper. Line a large plate with paper towels.

Once the oil is heated, place the biscuits in the oil two at a time—if you do more you will lower the temperature of the oil, and you don't want that. Fry the biscuits 3 to 4 minutes per side or until they are a deep golden brown. Remove and place them on the paper towel–lined plate. Repeat until you have fried all the donuts. Let them cool for 5 minutes while you make the glaze.

To make the glaze: In a medium bowl, whisk together the powdered sugar, vanilla and 2 tablespoons (30 ml) of milk until smooth. If the glaze seems too thick, add the other tablespoon (15 ml) of milk. Divide the glaze into two bowls that are wider than the donuts. Mix some pink food coloring into one bowl and leave the other one white.

Dip each donut into the glaze (pink or white). Let it sit for just a minute (not any longer, as the glaze will start to set), then garnish each with a Circus Animal Cookie and some nonpareils, if using. Set the donuts aside for the glaze to set.

Once the glaze has set (about 10 to 15 minutes), poke a hole or cut a slit in the bottom of each donut. Using your finger or a knife, hollow out some of the donut. With your piping bag, squeeze some filling into the hole in each donut.

The Bavarian cream you can keep in the fridge for up to 1 week. The donuts are best eaten the day of.

NOTES: I get it, frying is scary. The most important thing to remember is to constantly check the temperature of the oil (use a digital thermometer) to make sure it stays at 375°F (190°C). If it gets too hot it will brown the donuts too quickly and leave the inside raw. You can add a little more oil and it will cool the temperature down a bit. If it goes too low they will eventually cook but will have soaked up a ton of grease, so turn up the heat a bit.

You will have leftover Bavarian cream which you can just eat as a dessert itself.

DONUTS

3 cups (720 ml) canola oil

2 (8-count) packages Pillsbury Grands! Flaky Layers Original Biscuits

GLAZE

1½ cups (180 g) powdered sugar

1 tsp vanilla extract

2–3 tbsp (30–45 ml) milk

Pink food coloring

Circus Animal Cookies, for garnish

Rainbow nonpareils, for garnish (optional)

CRACKER JACK CUPCAKES

Cracker Jack is an American icon. I mean, you are *supposed* to have peanuts and Cracker Jack at the ball game . . . it's in the song they sing at every game. Many people wrongly assume Cracker Jack is caramel corn. It's actually molasses-based candy-coated popcorn and peanuts (all three of them in one box). Of course, as a kid the best thing about Cracker Jack, besides the sugar, was the prize in the box. Which was usually a temporary tattoo, and I was never quite skilled enough to get the whole thing on my hand. So I would have three-quarters of a fake tattoo on. I would then try to scare my parents into thinking their eight-year-old went and got three-quarters of a tattoo on her hand. They were always nice and played along, pretending to be surprised that it was fake after I told them. Sadly, now all you get is an online code to go play games. Anyway, to honor this icon I made a molasses cupcake that is infused with Cracker Jack and topped with a brown sugar Swiss meringue buttercream frosting.

To make the Cracker Jack milk: Put the Cracker Jack and the milk in a small saucepan and bring to a boil over medium-high heat, about 2 or 3 minutes. Remove from the heat as soon as it starts to boil, cover and set aside for 20 minutes for the milk to steep in the Cracker Jack. Then strain out the Cracker Jack pieces so there is just flavored milk. Discard the Cracker Jack pieces.

To make the cupcakes: Preheat the oven to 350°F (175°C). Position a rack in the middle of the oven. Line two 12-cup muffin tins with cupcake liners.

Melt the butter in the microwave at 60 percent power for 1½ to 2 minutes, then cover the bowl to keep the butter warm.

Using a stand mixer with the paddle attachment, beat the eggs on medium-low speed for 2 minutes, until they're light yellow and a bit foamy. Increase the mixer speed to medium-high and slowly pour the warm butter into the eggs, so that the mixture tempers and the eggs do not scramble. When all the butter is added, reduce the speed to medium-low. With the mixer running, add the sour cream, Cracker Jack milk, molasses, vanilla and salt. Mix for 1 minute until everything is well combined. Add the flour, sugar, baking powder and brown sugar to the batter. Mix on medium until everything is just combined, about 30 seconds. Scrape down the sides and bottom of the bowl, then mix for another 30 seconds.

Scoop the batter into the prepared muffin tins, filling them two-thirds of the way. Bake for 20 to 25 minutes, rotating the pan halfway through. The cupcakes are done when the centers spring back when you touch them. Remove the cupcakes from the oven. Take them out of the pan, and set them on a wire rack and let them cool completely while you make the frosting.

(continued)

YIELD
Makes 24

CRACKER JACK MILK

1 cup (56 g) Cracker Jack, plus more for garnish

1 cup (240 ml) whole milk

CUPCAKES

¾ cup (170 g) unsalted butter

4 large eggs

½ cup (120 ml) sour cream

½ cup (120 ml) Cracker Jack milk

⅓ cup (80 ml) molasses

1 tsp vanilla extract

1 tsp salt

2 cups (250 g) all-purpose flour

1 cup (200 g) granulated sugar

2 tsp (9 g) baking powder

1 cup (220 g) packed brown sugar

CRACKER JACK CUPCAKES (CONTINUED)

To make the frosting: Fill a small saucepan with 2 inches (5 cm) of water and bring it to a simmer. Put the egg whites, salt and dark brown sugar in the metal bowl of a stand mixer, and set the bowl over the pot of simmering water (the bowl should not touch the water). Heat, stirring occasionally, until the mixture reaches 150 to 160°F (65 to 71°C).

Transfer the bowl to the stand mixer with the whisk attachment. Beat on high speed until medium stiff peaks form, about 8 minutes. It should be thick and glossy. Reduce the mixer speed to medium-low and add the butter 1 tablespoon (14 g) at a time, letting it incorporate into the frosting for a few moments before adding more. At this point you might start to panic because it looks curdled or like it's not coming together. Don't worry. Just keep adding butter—it will come together. When all of the butter has been added and is incorporated (meaning you see no visible pieces of butter), turn the mixer up to high and whisk the frosting for about 3 to 5 minutes. It will be fluffy and smooth.

Use a pastry bag to pipe the frosting onto the cooled cupcakes, or spread it on with a knife. Top with Cracker Jack pieces.

NOTE: You are going to look at the frosting recipe and think it's a typo that there are 3 cups (680 g, 6 sticks) of butter in the recipe. That is not a typo. It's Swiss meringue BUTTERcream, and it's glorious.

FROSTING

1 cup (120 ml) egg whites (about 9)

¼ tsp salt

2 cups (440 g) packed dark brown sugar

3 cups (680 g) unsalted butter, at room temperature

SNICKERDOODLE COOKIE DOUGH RICE KRISPIES TREATS

YIELD
Makes about 12

I originally made these snickerdoodle truffles for my matron of honor, Laurie. Ours is an unusual friendship. How unusual? The *Chicago Tribune* featured our story (though neither of us live in Chicago). Why? Because I met her in person for the first time when she came to stay at my house a few days before my wedding. She lives across the country; I met her online. She was a fan of my blog, and she ran the baking group Tuesdays with Dorie (Greenspan). We bonded over hockey and baking. She loves all things snickerdoodle and is always wanting me to make as many things with snickerdoodle as I can. So I invented these cookie dough truffles for her—but I'm taking it up a notch and putting them into Rice Krispies treats, which is even better.

To make the cinnamon sugar: Put the sugar and cinnamon in a medium bowl and whisk until the cinnamon is evenly dispersed throughout the sugar. Set aside.

To make the truffles: In a medium bowl, mix together the flour, nutmeg, cinnamon, salt and cream of tartar. Set aside.

In the bowl of a stand mixer with the paddle attachment, cream together the butter and brown sugar until it's light and fluffy, about 3 minutes. Beat in the vanilla extract for another 30 seconds. With the speed on low, slowly add the flour mixture, alternating with the condensed milk, and beating well after each addition. (This is just like making regular snickerdoodles but you replace the eggs with condensed milk.) It will have the same consistency as regular cookie dough.

Shape the dough into 1-inch (2.5-cm) balls. Roll them in the cinnamon sugar, just as you would with a snickerdoodle cookie. Then place them in an airtight container and put them in the freezer for at least 3 hours. How many cookie dough balls you get really depends on what you think a 1-inch (2.5-cm) ball looks like. I have found that varies greatly. You will have leftover truffles. You can eat them as is or toss them on ice cream. Or in oatmeal if you are feeling healthy.

To make the Rice Krispies treats: Butter a 9 x 13–inch (23 x 33–cm) pan and sprinkle in the cinnamon sugar. Move the pan around to make sure the bottom and sides are coated. Set aside.

Melt the butter in a large saucepan over low heat, then add the marshmallows and vanilla. Stir until the marshmallows begin to melt, about 2 or 3 minutes. Stir in the Rice Krispies so they are completely coated with marshmallow mixture. Remove from the heat. Fold the snickerdoodle truffles into the marshmallow mixture. Press the mixture into the prepared pan and press down with your hands to make the top as flat as possible. Let it sit for about 30 minutes before cutting into squares.

CINNAMON SUGAR

1 cup (200 g) granulated sugar

¼ cup (31 g) ground cinnamon

SNICKERDOODLE COOKIE DOUGH TRUFFLES

2 cups (250 g) all-purpose flour

½ tsp freshly ground nutmeg

½ tsp ground cinnamon

½ tsp salt

1 tsp cream of tartar

½ cup (114 g) unsalted butter, at room temperature

¾ cup (165 g) packed brown sugar

1 tsp vanilla extract

1 (14-oz [397-g]) can sweetened condensed milk

TREATS

6 tbsp (85 g) unsalted butter, plus some for greasing

⅓ cup (66 g) cinnamon sugar

1 (16-ounce [454-g]) bag mini marshmallows

½ tsp vanilla extract

12 oz (340 g) Rice Krispies cereal

20–30 snickerdoodle cookie dough truffles

OATMEAL COOKIE CREAM PIE PIE

YIELD
Serves about 8

I'm not sure who decided to take two oatmeal cookies and stuff them with vanilla marshmallow cream, but they are definitely a reminder that not all heroes wear capes—some work at snack factories. I love me a cookie pie, and the addition of the filling just makes for an ooey, gooey pie of goodness. You can serve it plain or with ice cream. I suggest cinnamon ice cream. Move over Little Debbie, here comes Not So Little Peabody.

To make the cream pie filling: In the bowl of a stand mixer with the paddle attachment, cream the shortening, mascarpone cheese, powdered sugar and vanilla together until they're smooth. Add the marshmallow creme and flour and mix until they're fully combined. Scrape everything into a medium bowl, cover with plastic wrap and place in the fridge until you're ready to use it.

To make the cookie pie: Grease a 9-inch (23-cm) pie plate with butter. Roll out the pie crust and gently place it in the pie pan. Use your fingers to pinch the edges of the crust all around, crimping them evenly (as best you can). Place the pie crust in the fridge until you're ready to use it.

Preheat the oven to 350°F (175°C).

In a large bowl, mix the sugar, brown sugar, flour and salt. Add the eggs one at a time, scraping the bottom and sides of the bowl after each egg. Slowly pour the melted butter into the sugar mixture and whisk until smooth. Fold in the oats until they are evenly distributed.

Pour half the cookie pie batter into the chilled pie crust. Bake for 10 minutes, then remove it from the oven.

Pour all the cream pie filling over the baked cookie pie batter. Using your hands or a spoon, drop the remaining cookie pie batter on top of the cream pie layer. Bake until the filling is slightly puffed and the center is set, about 40 to 45 minutes. Let it cool completely.

This pie will keep covered in the fridge for up to 3 days.

NOTES: This is a gooey pie. It will not be a hard cookie on the bottom. The filling is meant to be soft; it will not set like a cheesecake. The top of the pie, however, will be crispy. If you can't find mascarpone cheese you can use cream cheese, but the mascarpone really is better.

CREAM PIE FILLING

1 cup (200 g) shortening

½ cup (116 g) mascarpone cheese

1 cup (120 g) powdered sugar

1½ tsp (7 ml) vanilla extract

1 (7-oz [198-g]) jar marshmallow creme

1 tbsp (8 g) all-purpose flour

COOKIE PIE

½ cup (114 g) unsalted butter, melted and slightly cooled, plus more for greasing

1 bottom pie crust (recipe of your choice or store-bought)

½ cup (100 g) granulated sugar

¾ cup (165 g) packed brown sugar

½ cup (63 g) all-purpose flour

½ tsp salt

2 large eggs

1½ cups (135 g) old-fashioned rolled oats

HONEY BUNS BREAD PUDDING

YIELD
Serves about 8

Honey Buns—glazed cakes swirled with cinnamon and honey—are still one of my all-time favorites. If I'm not feeling well, I love to pop one in the microwave for 30 seconds and enjoy one—or six. Since bread pudding is my favorite dessert, it only made sense for me to make bread pudding using Honey Buns. To be honest, I have no idea why I hadn't done it before now.

Preheat the oven to 350°F (175°C). Spray an 8 x 8–inch (20 x 20–cm) pan with nonstick baking spray.

To make the bread pudding: In a large bowl, whisk together the eggs, yolk, cream, sugar and vanilla until they're fully combined. Spread half of the Honey Buns cubes over the bottom of the pan. Pour in half the custard mixture and press the bread down to soak up the custard. Spread the remaining Honey Buns cubes on top of the bottom layer. Pour on the remaining custard and again press the bread pieces down.

Cover the pan with foil and bake for 30 minutes. Remove the foil and bake for another 15 to 20 minutes, until none of the custard mixture is still liquid. Remove the pan from the oven and let it cool while you prepare the sauce.

To make the honey caramel sauce: In a medium saucepan, combine the honey, water and sugar. Heat over medium heat, swirling the pan, until the sugar is dissolved, about 2 to 3 minutes. Then bring the mixture to a boil and cook until it is a deep golden brown, 5 to 6 minutes. Remove from the heat and carefully whisk in the cream, butter, salt and vanilla. The mixture will spatter, so be careful.

Let the sauce cool to thicken. The honey caramel sauce can be served either warm or at room temperature. You can refrigerate it in an airtight container up to 2 weeks; gently reheat it before serving.

NOTE: You can serve this bread pudding with ice cream to make it extra special.

BREAD PUDDING

2 large eggs

1 egg yolk

1¼ cups (300 ml) heavy cream

½ cup (100 g) granulated sugar

½ tsp vanilla extract

10 Honey Buns, cut into large cubes

HONEY CARAMEL SAUCE

2 tbsp (30 ml) honey

2 tbsp (30 ml) water

½ cup (100 g) granulated sugar

½ cup (120 ml) heavy cream

2 tbsp (28 g) unsalted butter

¼ tsp salt

½ tsp vanilla extract

COSMIC BROWNIES TORTE

YIELD
Serves about 6

I did not join the Cosmic Brownies bandwagon until high school, when they were pretty much the only snack cake sold in the cafeteria. While my mom packed me a lunch every day, in order to pretend to be cool you had to buy something as well. I came to appreciate the ratio of chocolate frosting to brownie. Plus, who doesn't love rainbow chips?

To make the brownie rounds: Preheat the oven to 325°F (160°C). Spray four 4½-inch (11-cm)-diameter springform pans with nonstick baking spray.

In the bowl of a stand mixer with the paddle attachment, mix together the butter and sugar for about 2 minutes. Add the egg, egg yolk and vanilla. Beat another minute. Pour in the cocoa, flour, baking powder and salt, and mix on low speed until they're all fully incorporated. Turn off the mixer.

Fold in the chocolate chips until they're completely distributed throughout the brownie batter. Using a standard-sized (typically ½-cup [120-ml]) ice cream scoop, scoop 1½ scoops of batter into each pan. If there is any batter leftover, try to distribute it among the pans as evenly as possible. With a spatula, smooth and even out the batter in the pans.

Bake for 20 to 23 minutes. Remove the pans from the oven and let the brownie rounds cool in their pans.

To make the chocolate ganache: Place both kinds of chocolate chips in a medium heatproof bowl and set aside. In a small saucepan, bring the cream to a boil over medium-high heat. When it just starts to boil, pour the hot cream over the chocolate chips. Let them sit for 5 minutes, then whisk until the mixture is smooth and glossy.

To assemble the torte: Remove the brownie rounds from their springform pans. If they're still warm, place them in the freezer for about 10 minutes—you don't want them to melt the ganache.

Place one brownie round on a plate. With a knife or offset spatula, spread a quarter of the chocolate ganache on top. Sprinkle with 2 tablespoons (22 g) of rainbow chips. Place another brownie round on top of that. Spread another quarter of the ganache on that round and sprinkle with 2 tablespoons (22 g) of rainbow chips. Place the third brownie round on top of the second layer and add another quarter of the ganache and 2 tablespoons (22 g) of rainbow chips. Add the last brownie layer and spread the remaining ganache over the top of the torte. Add the remaining rainbow chips.

Let the torte set for about 30 minutes before serving.

BROWNIE ROUNDS

7 tbsp (98 g) unsalted butter

1 cup (200 g) granulated sugar

1 large egg

1 egg yolk

½ tsp vanilla extract

⅓ cup (29 g) unsweetened cocoa powder, sifted

½ cup (63 g) all-purpose flour

¼ tsp baking powder

⅛ tsp salt

½ cup (86 g) mini semisweet chocolate chips

CHOCOLATE GANACHE

4 oz (113 g) milk chocolate chips

4 oz (113 g) semisweet chocolate chips

½ cup (120 ml) heavy cream

3 oz (85 g) rainbow chocolate chips

SNOBALL SANDWICH COOKIES

YIELD
Makes about 24

In college I roomed with a Japanese exchange student for a semester. She was here on a program to learn English, and one time my mother sent a care package with treats, including Snoballs. Two of my friends and I couldn't stop laughing as I tried to explain what they were. To this day, I'm not sure she really understood my description. While oddly named, they are tasty all the same. I've turned those flavors into sandwich cookies, with a chocolate cookie base filled with a marshmallow filling and then rolled in pink coconut.

To make the chocolate cookies: In the bowl of a stand mixer with the paddle attachment, cream together the butter and sugar on medium speed until they're light and fluffy, about 3 minutes. Turn the mixer to low and add the egg and vanilla. Mix until they're just incorporated. With the mixer still on low, add in the flour 1 cup (125 g) at a time. Then mix in the cocoa powder and salt. Mix until the cocoa is completely incorporated, then turn off the mixer.

Set out a large piece of parchment paper or wax paper on the countertop and scrape all the dough onto it. Place another piece of parchment or wax paper on top, then roll out the dough to about ¼- to ½-inch (6- to 13-mm) thickness. Place the dough (still sandwiched in parchment) on a flat board or pan, and put it in the refrigerator for about 1 hour or the freezer for 15 minutes, until the dough is firm.

When you're ready to bake, preheat the oven to 350°F (175°C). Line a large cookie sheet with parchment paper. Remove the dough and peel the parchment paper off one side. Using a round cookie cutter (I used a 1¾-inch [4.5-cm] cutter), cut out the cookies and place on the prepared cookie sheet. After you have cut out all your cookies, stick the dough scraps back together, and roll it out again. Cut out as many cookies as you can.

Bake the cookies for 12 to 14 minutes; you want them to be crisp. Cool the cookies on a wire rack to room temperature.

To make the marshmallow filling: In the bowl of a stand mixer, beat the butter until it's fluffy, about 3 minutes. Add the marshmallow creme and beat again, scraping the sides and bottom of the bowl as needed. Add the powdered sugar and mix well, about 2 to 3 minutes, making sure to scrape down the sides and bottom of the bowl. The texture should be light and fluffy. Put the coconut in a medium bowl and tint it with a drop of pink food coloring (gel works better than liquid). Mix well using a fork—or your fingers if you don't mind pink fingertips. Set aside.

To assemble the cookies: Lay out your cookies and match each cookie with a partner cookie that looks to be the same thickness. Spread a generous scoop (or pipe) of the filling onto one of the cookies and sandwich it with its partner. Give it a light squeeze. Then roll the sides of the sandwich cookies in the pink coconut so it sticks to the outer edges of the filling.

CHOCOLATE COOKIES

1 cup (227 g) unsalted butter, at room temperature

1¼ cups (250 g) granulated sugar

1 large egg

1 tsp vanilla extract

2 cups (250 g) all-purpose flour

1 cup (88 g) unsweetened cocoa powder

Pinch of salt

MARSHMALLOW FILLING

1½ cups (341 g) unsalted butter, softened

1 (13-oz [368-g]) jar marshmallow creme

1 cup (120 g) powdered sugar

1 cup (93 g) sweetened flaked coconut

Pink soft gel food coloring

NOTE: I like to chop the coconut into finer pieces than what comes out of the bag. I find that, for this recipe, having the smaller flakes of coconut helps it stick when you're rolling the filling in it.

CHOCOLATE CHIP COOKIE TIRAMISU

YIELD
Serves 8

To say that Italian grandmothers are rolling over in their graves about this recipe is putting it mildly. Not only is using chocolate chip cookies so very *not* Italian, but neither is the method I use to make the filling. True tiramisu does not use cooked eggs—they are raw. Which I have found a lot of people are not big fans of, and I don't blame them. I cook both the yolks and the egg white mixture in this recipe. The result—a light and fluffy filling—is the same, so I think it works fine. Italian grandmothers, on the other hand, will probably disagree.

To make the filling: Fill a small saucepan with 2 inches (5 cm) of water and bring it to a simmer. Using the bowl of a stand mixer, mix the egg, egg yolks and ½ cup (100 g) of sugar. Set the bowl over the gently simmering water and stir until the sugar has dissolved and the mixture has reached 145°F (63°C), about 5 minutes. Remove the bowl but leave the water gently simmering.

Transfer the bowl to the mixer fitted with the whisk attachment and whip on high speed until it turns thick and pale, about 3 minutes. Add the mascarpone cheese and beat until it is fully combined. Transfer the mixture to a large bowl. Clean the mixing bowl.

In the clean mixing bowl, mix the egg whites and the remaining ½ cup (100 g) of sugar. Set the bowl over the gently simmering water and stir until the sugar has dissolved and the mixture has reached 160°F (71°C), about 4 to 6 minutes.

Transfer the bowl to the mixer and, using the whisk attachment, whip the egg white mixture on a high speed until the mixture becomes thick but does not turn glossy, about 5 minutes. You want stiff peaks but you do not want it to turn into meringue. Fold the whipped egg white mixture into the egg yolk and mascarpone mixture. Then fold in the semisweet chocolate.

To make the tiramisu: Spread a thin layer (about ¼ cup [60 ml]) of the filling on the bottom of a 8 x 8–inch (20 x 20–cm) clear glass pan (it doesn't have to be glass, but you can see the layers that way). Layer 12 chocolate chip cookies over the filling. They will not all fit perfectly (round cookies, square pan) and you will need to break some of them to fit; that's fine. Brush the tops of the cookies with some espresso. (Don't dip them, like traditional tiramisu, or the cookies will get too soggy). Spread about ½ cup (120 ml) of the filling over the cookies. Then add another layer of 12 cookies, and brush them with espresso. Then filling. Then cookies. Then espresso. Then filling. Then cookies. Then espresso. And finally filling.

Cover the dish with plastic wrap and chill in the fridge for at least 4 hours. The longer it sits, the more it will firm up. I prefer overnight.

Before serving, mix the espresso powder, cocoa powder and powdered sugar together. Dust the tiramisu with the mixture. Top with extra chocolate chip cookies, if desired.

FILLING

1 large egg

3 egg yolks

1 cup (200 g) granulated sugar, divided

2 cups (464 g) mascarpone cheese, at room temperature

3 egg whites

¼ cup (43 g) finely chopped semi-sweet chocolate

TIRAMISU

48 Chips Ahoy! chocolate chip cookies, plus more for garnish

6 tbsp (90 ml) brewed espresso or coffee

TOPPING

1 tsp espresso powder

1 tbsp (6 g) unsweetened cocoa powder

¼ cup (30 g) powdered sugar

TWINKIE WHOOPIE PIES

YIELD
Makes 16 to 18

To me there is nothing more iconic than the Twinkie. No one ever seems to want to admit to eating them, and yet when I bring a couple of boxes to a hockey tournament they are gone by the end of the first game. So someone is eating them. Me, I love a frozen Twinkie. If you have never tried it that way, I highly suggest it. I tried many different variations on making this whoopie pie, and the only way to get a true Twinkie flavor is to use boxed yellow cake mix.

To make the Twinkie cookies: Preheat the oven to 350°F (175°C). Line a large cookie sheet with parchment paper.

In the bowl of a stand mixer with the paddle attachment, beat the cake mix, butter, water and eggs on low until they're combined, about 30 seconds, scraping the sides and bottom of the bowl to incorporate everything. Increase the speed to medium and beat for an additional 1 minute. Drop 1½ to 2 tablespoons (23 to 30 g) of dough (I use a cookie scoop) onto the prepared baking sheet, spaced about 2 inches (5 cm) apart. You will have more dough than you can bake on one sheet.

Bake for about 10 minutes, or until the Twinkie cookies are lightly golden brown on the edges and set in the center. Remove them to a wire rack to cool, and repeat with the remaining dough.

To make the filling: In a medium mixing bowl, combine the shortening, marshmallow creme, sugar, vanilla and 2 teaspoons (10 ml) of milk and mix until smooth. If the filling is too thick to spread, add more milk 1 teaspoon at a time.

To assemble the pies: Turn half the cookies over and spread about 2 tablespoons (30 ml) of filling over the flat side. Top with another cookie, flat side down, and lightly press them together.

TWINKIE COOKIES

1 (15.25-oz [432-g]) boxed yellow cake mix

½ cup (114 g) unsalted butter, melted

½ cup (120 ml) water

3 large eggs

FILLING

½ cup (100 g) vegetable shortening

1 cup (96 g) marshmallow creme

2 cups (240 g) powdered sugar

1 tsp vanilla extract

2–4 tsp (10–20 ml) whole milk

CHILL OUT

RECIPES INSPIRED BY
MY FAVORITE ICE CREAM FLAVORS

No matter what you were doing as a kid, if you heard the ice cream man you dropped everything and immediately ran to your house to beg for money—and hoped your parents would give in. My dad usually would if I offered to bring him back something. He was a Creamsicle guy back then.

Then you had to listen and figure out where the ice cream man was in the neighborhood, because you couldn't pin your hopes on him stopping on your street. And then you ran. And ran. And ran. I wouldn't be surprised if on average I ran at least a half a mile every time he came around—which was every summer day when I was a kid. That was the way to have ice cream, because you got your exercise too. Now it's just a walk from my couch to my fridge . . . and I have a very tiny house.

When I finally found the ice cream truck, I would stare at the menu and all its possibilities. My parents were generous, so price was not usually a factor in picking. In fact, they often gave me some extra in case there was a kid there who didn't have any money. They were nice like that; still are. Hey Mom and Dad, can you send me some ice cream money?

Despite all the options, I almost always went with the Drumstick. It's just so classic. You get your vanilla ice cream, some chocolate, nuts and, of course, a cone. Practically perfect.

While the flavors are unlimited these days, in this chapter I tried to stick with some of the more tried and true ice cream flavors. With the exception of the Atlantic Beach Pie Thumbprint Cookies (page 53), which I made with my husband in mind because he is usually the adventurous one when we go to get ice cream. Drumstick Ice Cream Sweet Rolls (page 37) are for me. They have vanilla ice cream in the rolls and the glaze, plus pieces of ice cream cone, nuts and chocolate. Yum!

Butter Pecan Ice Cream Caramels (page 40) are for my mom because that's her go-to ice cream and she likes caramels. You literally use melted ice cream to make the caramels. Mint Chocolate Chip Cupcakes (page 49) are for my dad—though this time in cupcake form. Mint chocolate chip ice cream is in the cupcake batter, plus it has a light and fluffy Swiss meringue buttercream and is dipped in mint white chocolate and topped with mini chocolate chips! How fun is that?

Banana splits, hot fudge sundaes, root beer floats, cookies and cream . . . they are all in here in one dessert form or another.

HOT FUDGE SUNDAE LAYER CAKE

YIELD
Serves 8 to 10

This is an amazing cake that has vanilla ice cream in the cake *and* the frosting! All topped with hot fudge, whipped cream, sprinkles (which are for winners) and maraschino cherries. It's every ten-year-old's (and wannabe ten-year-old's) perfect cake. This recipe uses custard buttercream, also known as German buttercream. What makes it so great is that it's not a very sweet frosting, which works perfectly for this cake since you are also covering it in hot fudge sauce.

To make the cake: Preheat the oven to 350°F (175°C). Place a rack one-third of the way from the bottom of the oven and a second rack two-thirds from the bottom. Line three 9-inch (23-cm) round cake pans with parchment paper circles and spray with nonstick baking spray.

In a medium bowl, combine the flour, baking soda, salt and baking powder. Set aside.

In a small bowl, mix together the buttermilk and melted ice cream and set aside.

In the bowl of a stand mixer with the paddle attachment, beat the butter and sugar on medium speed until they're light and fluffy, about 2 minutes. Scrape down the sides and bottom of the bowl and add the egg whites and vanilla. Beat on medium speed for 1 minute. Add one-third of the flour mixture and beat on medium speed until it's incorporated. Add half the buttermilk and ice cream mixture and beat on medium until it's mixed in. Scrape down the sides and bottom of the bowl and add another third of the flour mixture and the rest of the buttermilk and ice cream mixture, beating between each addition. Finish with the remaining third of the flour mixture and beat until it's incorporated. The batter will be thick and glossy.

Pour the batter evenly into the prepared pans. I like to use an ice cream scoop because the batter is so thick. Set two cake pans on one of the oven racks and the third pan on the other rack, staggering them so the cakes are not directly over one another. Bake for 25 to 35 minutes, until the tops are flat and browned. Cool the cakes in their pans for 10 minutes, then invert them onto racks to cool completely. The cakes can be wrapped in plastic wrap and frozen for up to 3 weeks.

To make the vanilla ice cream custard buttercream: In a large heatproof bowl, whisk together the sugar, cornstarch, egg, egg yolks and salt. The mixture will be thick and look grainy from the sugar. Set it aside.

In a medium nonstick saucepan, heat the melted ice cream, milk and vanilla bean paste to just shy of a simmer—so just starting to form bubbles. Remove from the heat. Using one hand to whisk constantly, pour about ½ cup (120 ml) of the hot milk and ice cream mixture into the egg mixture. This helps to temper the eggs and prevent them from scrambling. Add an additional ½ cup (120 ml) of hot milk and ice cream to the egg mixture, whisking the whole time until it's fully incorporated.

(continued)

CAKE

3 cups (360 g) cake flour

¾ tsp baking soda

¾ tsp salt

1½ tsp (7 g) baking powder

¾ cup (180 ml) buttermilk

¾ cup (180 ml) melted vanilla ice cream

1½ cups (341 g) unsalted butter, at room temperature

2⅓ cups (466 g) granulated sugar

3 egg whites

1 tsp vanilla extract

VANILLA ICE CREAM CUSTARD BUTTERCREAM

1¼ cups (250 g) granulated sugar

3 tbsp (24 g) cornstarch

1 large egg

2 egg yolks

⅛ tsp salt

1 cup (240 ml) melted vanilla ice cream

½ cup (120 ml) whole milk

1 tbsp (15 ml) vanilla bean paste

3 cups (681 g) unsalted butter, at room temperature, divided

HOT FUDGE SUNDAE LAYER CAKE (CONTINUED)

Then pour the egg and milk mixture back into the saucepan. Heat it over medium heat, whisking constantly but slowly, because if you whisk too quickly it won't thicken. Whisk until it begins to bubble—they are kind of big bubbles that sometimes make a burping sound. This might take about 2 to 3 minutes. Be ready, as it will thicken quickly. Once it has thickened, cook for 1 minute, then remove the saucepan from the heat. Pour the mixture into a shallow dish such as a pie pan (the shallower the pan, the quicker it will cool off—physics), and press some plastic wrap over the surface to prevent a skin forming. Refrigerate until it's cold.

In the bowl of a stand mixer with the paddle attachment, beat 2 cups (454 g) of butter until it's smooth. Scrape it all out of the mixing bowl into a dish and set aside.

Add the whisk attachment to the mixer and, using the same bowl you just mixed the butter in (no need to clean it), whip the cold buttercream mixture on medium until it's creamy and lump-free. Add the butter you just whipped and mix on low until it's incorporated. Now begin adding the remaining 1 cup (227 g) of butter, a few pieces at a time, until it's fully incorporated. Switch to the paddle attachment and beat for a few minutes, until the buttercream is smooth and silky.

You are probably going to freak a little when you start making this. It will look curdled and you will panic that you wasted all those ingredients. You need to just put your splash guard on your mixer and dial it up to high and let it go. It does come together. I promise. Mine took about 5 minutes of really beating to come together. The buttercream should be super smooth when you're done.

To make the hot fudge sauce: Bring the cream, corn syrup, brown sugar, cocoa, salt and half the chocolate to a boil in a 1½-quart (1.4-L) heavy saucepan over medium heat, stirring, until the chocolate is melted, about 3 minutes. Reduce the heat and cook at a low boil, stirring occasionally, for 5 minutes. Remove the pan from the heat. Add the butter, vanilla and the remaining chocolate and stir until you have a smooth sauce. Let it cool down so you don't melt the buttercream when you assemble the cake.

To assemble the cake: Level the cake layers using a cake leveler or a bread knife. Place the first cake layer on a turntable or cake stand. Smooth a thick layer of buttercream over the cake using an offset spatula. Place the second cake layer on top, and again smooth a layer of buttercream on top of the cake. Place the final cake layer on top, making sure the edges are straight and aligned. Using an offset spatula, give the whole cake a thin coating of buttercream. Put the cake in the fridge for 20 to 30 minutes to let the frosting set a little.

Follow with one more layer of buttercream frosting. It will be a thin coat and it's fine if you see the cake through the layers. Pour 1 cup (240 ml) of the hot fudge sauce on top of the cake and smooth it out so it falls down the sides of the cake. You can use as much of the hot fudge sauce as you like. Garnish the cake with whipped cream, sprinkles and maraschino cherries.

HOT FUDGE SAUCE

⅔ cup (160 ml) heavy cream

½ cup (120 ml) light corn syrup

⅓ cup (73 g) packed dark brown sugar

¼ cup (22 g) unsweetened Dutch-process cocoa powder

¼ tsp salt

6 oz (170 g) fine-quality semisweet chocolate, finely chopped, divided

2 tbsp (28 g) unsalted butter

1 tsp vanilla extract

Whipped cream, for garnish

Sprinkles, for garnish

Maraschino cherries, for garnish

DRUMSTICK ICE CREAM SWEET ROLLS

YIELD
Makes 12 large rolls

I have a major weakness for Drumstick ice cream cones. Major. If I buy a box for home, the kind that has four servings in it, it becomes one serving. Which is why I never buy the family pack. These sweet rolls are a great way to have ice cream for breakfast. Big puffy yeast rolls filled with crushed sugar cones, chocolate and peanuts all topped with vanilla ice cream glaze—clearly the breakfast of champions.

To make the dough: In the bowl of a stand mixer with the paddle attachment, add the warm water, yeast and ½ teaspoon of sugar. Let the yeast proof for 5 to 10 minutes—the mixture will puff up. (If it does not then your yeast is bad and the rolls won't rise, so best to throw the yeast mixture out and start again with new yeast.) While you're waiting, oil a large bowl with vegetable oil, and set aside.

After the yeast gets bubbly and puffy, add the buttermilk, melted ice cream, eggs, ½ cup (100 g) of sugar, salt, vanilla and melted butter, and mix with the paddle attachment until they're fully combined. Add in 2½ cups (343 g) of the flour and mix until the dough is fully combined.

Switch to a hook attachment, then add another 1 cup (137 g) of flour and knead on low speed until the dough is combined. Continue to knead for about 5 or 6 minutes, adding a little more flour as needed to end up with a soft and moist dough. The dough shouldn't stick to the sides of the bowl, but will stick to the bottom.

Transfer the dough to the oiled bowl, cover with plastic wrap (I find Glad Press'n Seal works best) and let rise in a warm place until it's doubled in volume, about 1½ hours.

While the dough is rising, make the filling. In a large bowl mix together the crushed cones, chocolate and peanuts. Set aside. In a small bowl mix together the butter and warm melted ice cream—the ice cream must be warm or it will cause the butter to seize up. Set aside.

To make the sweet rolls: Punch down the dough after it has doubled in volume. Spray a 9 x 13–inch (23 x 33–cm) pan with nonstick baking spray. Lightly dust a working surface with flour and turn the dough out onto it. Sprinkle the top of the dough with a little flour, then roll the dough out into an 18 x 20–inch (45 x 50–cm) rectangle.

Spoon and spread the filling evenly over the rolled-out dough. Try to leave a ½-inch (13-mm) border uncovered all around the edges. Beginning on the shorter side, tightly roll the dough into a cylinder. Pinch the seam along the length of the cylinder to seal it. (Brushing a little egg white underneath helps, if needed, but I just use a toothpick on the cut rolls that aren't cooperating and staying sealed.) Use a large, sharp knife to cut the cylinder into 12 equal portions—they should each be about 1½ inches (4 cm) long.

(continued)

DOUGH

½ cup (120 ml) water, warm (110–115°F [43–46°C])

1 tbsp (9 g) active dry yeast

½ cup (100 g) plus ½ tsp granulated sugar, divided

¼ cup (60 ml) buttermilk, at room temperature

¼ cup (60 ml) melted vanilla ice cream, at room temperature

2 large eggs

1 tsp salt

1 tsp vanilla bean paste or extract

6 tbsp (84 g) unsalted butter, melted and slightly cooled

3½–4 cups (480–548 g) bread flour, divided

FILLING

3 sugar or waffle cones, finely crushed, plus more for garnish (optional)

1 cup (168 g) finely chopped milk chocolate, plus more for garnish (optional)

½ cup (70 g) chopped unsalted roasted peanuts, plus more for garnish (optional)

5 tbsp (70 g) unsalted butter, at room temperature

¼ cup (60 ml) melted vanilla ice cream, warm

DRUMSTICK ICE CREAM SWEET ROLLS (CONTINUED)

Arrange the rolls on your prepared pan, spacing them evenly apart. Cover loosely with plastic wrap, and let the rolls rise in a warm place until they have doubled in volume, about 1½ hours.

In the last 20 minutes of rising time, preheat the oven to 350°F (175°C).

Bake the rolls about 25 to 30 minutes, until the centers are no longer doughy. Remove them from the oven and set them on a wire rack to cool while you make the glaze.

To make the glaze: In a small saucepan over low heat, warm the butter and melted ice cream, stirring occasionally, until the butter is melted and the liquid is gently simmering, about 2 minutes. Remove the pan from the heat, add the powdered sugar and use a small rubber spatula to stir the icing until it's thick and creamy.

Using a small spoon, drizzle about 1 tablespoon (15 ml) of the icing onto the center of each roll and use the back of the spoon to spread the icing over the tops of the rolls. Garnish with crushed cone pieces, chopped peanuts and chopped chocolate, if using.

GLAZE

2 tbsp (28 g) unsalted butter, melted

¾ cup (180 ml) melted vanilla ice cream

3 cups (360 g) powdered sugar

BUTTER PECAN ICE CREAM CARAMELS

YIELD
Makes about 32

I had wondered for years what would happen if I melted ice cream and turned it into caramels—and one day I did it. It took a lot of tries. A lot. Caramels are already buttery, so making butter pecan caramels just made sense. The key is to make sure you get a premium ice cream—one where cream is listed as the first ingredient. With this recipe, I will just say: Be patient. This one is hard for people. Candy making takes time. I taught junior high school for years, so I have a lot of patience.

¼ cup (60 ml) heavy cream

¾ cup (180 ml) melted butter pecan ice cream

4 tbsp (57 g) unsalted butter

¼ tsp salt

1½ cups (288 g) superfine sugar

4 tbsp (60 ml) Lyle's Golden Syrup (or light corn syrup)

4 tbsp (60 ml) water

½ tsp vanilla extract

⅓ cup (36 g) chopped pecans

Line an 8 x 8–inch (20 x 20–cm) pan with parchment paper and spray it with nonstick baking spray.

In a 2-cup (480-ml) glass measuring cup, add the cream, melted ice cream, butter and salt. Microwave in 30-second pulses until everything is melted and steaming. Set aside.

In a 2-quart (2-L) saucepan (seriously, don't use a smaller one—it boils up and it's not fun to clean up), add the sugar, Lyle's Golden Syrup and water. Turn the heat to high and cook without stirring until it reaches 290 to 295°F (143 to 146°C). Turn the heat off.

Slowly pour in the cream mixture in a steady stream and whisk gently. Turn the heat back to high and cook without stirring until it reaches 250°F (120°C). Turn off the heat, add the vanilla and fold in the pecan pieces. Whisk gently to combine. Immediately pour the mixture into the prepared pan; *do not* scrape the bottom of the pot.

Let the caramel sit at room temperature for a few hours, or overnight. Don't try to rush the process by putting it in the fridge or the caramel will crystalize and not have the desired texture. When it has firmed up, slice the caramel into the shapes you like and wrap each piece individually in wax paper.

NOTES: A good thermometer will really help with the recipe. I prefer a digital laser thermometer.

Have all your ingredients out and measured before you start. Candy making is about timing, and if you have to measure as you go there is a good chance things won't turn out.

Don't stir. You will want to, but don't do it and don't scrape the bottom of the saucepan. Often in the caramelization process the candy on the bottom of the pan will get more brown than you want. Don't scrape that out. Just let whatever caramel comes out . . . come out.

Don't touch. You may be tempted to stick your finger in there to see how it tastes. It tastes like burnt fingers if you stick your finger in there.

ROOT BEER FLOAT MINI CONES

YIELD
Makes 25

My food blogger friend Erin (The Spiffy Cookie) is a big root beer fan. I don't say that lightly. I've never met someone more into root beer in my life. Her hobby is collecting root beers from everywhere. Where I live just happens to have an all-root beer store. There are actually three locations. Who knew root beer was so popular? Anyway, Erin found out about the store and we planned a whole trip around her coming out to get root beer. She, fellow blogger Kita (Pass the Sushi), my husband and I ate our way through most of the Seattle area that weekend . . . and purchased a lot of root beer. A *lot* of root beer. These mini cones, which are filled with a root beer condensed milk filling, are in honor of Erin and her obsession.

3 cups (720 ml) root beer

25 mini ice cream cones with flat bottoms

2 (14-oz [397-g]) cans sweetened condensed milk

½ cup (120 ml) sour cream

25 mini scoops vanilla ice cream

Place the root beer in a medium saucepan and bring it to a boil over medium-high heat. Once it's boiling, reduce the heat to medium and simmer until the liquid has been reduced by half, about 20 to 25 minutes. You need to keep an eye on it or it can burn. (And let me tell you from experience that getting burned soda off the bottom of your pan is super fun.) Take the pan off the stove and let it cool. The syrup will thicken as it cools.

Preheat the oven to 350°F (175°C). Place the ice cream cones, open side up, on a large baking sheet.

In a medium bowl, whisk together the sweetened condensed milk, ¾ cup (180 ml) of the root beer syrup you just made, and the sour cream until everything is fully incorporated and smooth. Place the mixture in a large measuring cup that has a pour spout. Carefully pour the mixture into the cones until they are filled to the top. They don't rise much, so it's fine to fill them all the way. Bake for 5 to 8 minutes. You want them set with just a tiny hint of a wiggle in the middle.

Remove the cones from the oven and let them cool to room temperature. Transfer to the fridge and chill for 3 hours. To serve, top each cone with a mini scoop of vanilla ice cream.

NOTE: You can do this with any soda. Cola is good. Orange soda is good. Cream soda is good. The possibilities are actually quite extensive with all the soda flavors they have these days. But promise me you won't make this with turkey and gravy soda (yes, it's a real thing).

COOKIES AND CREAM ICE CREAM BREAD PUDDING

YIELD
Serves 6 to 8

Right after vanilla and chocolate, the most popular ice cream flavor is cookies and cream. And why wouldn't it be? I mean its vanilla ice cream with chopped up chocolate creme sandwich cookies. My gripe though is most commercial ice creams do not have nearly enough cookie pieces and I always end up adding more. This recipe not only uses melted cookies and cream ice cream in it but you actually scrape out the Oreo filling and use it as part of the custard which makes it extra fantastic.

To make the bread pudding: Preheat the oven to 350°F (175°C). Spray a square baking pan with nonstick baking spray. I use a 9 x 9–inch (23 x 23–cm) pan, but you can use an 8 x 8–inch (20 x 20–cm) or 10 x 10–inch (25 x 25–cm) pan— basically whatever pan will hold the amount of bread you have.

Unscrew the Oreos and scrape all the filling into a large microwave-safe bowl. Crush the chocolate cookies into coarse crumbs.

Spread half the bread cubes in the baking dish. Sprinkle half the crushed Oreo cookies over the bread. Add the remaining half of the bread and top with the remaining half of the crushed cookies.

Heat the Oreo filling in the microwave for 45 seconds, then whisk until it's smooth. Mix in the egg yolks, eggs and salt. Then whisk in the cream and melted ice cream and beat until everything is fully incorporated.

Pour the custard over the bread. Press down the bread pieces with your hands until the bread is soaked with the custard. You may have extra custard, depending on how stale your bread is. Don't feel like you have to use all the custard.

Cover the bread pudding with foil. Then place the pan into another baking pan big enough to hold it without touching the sides. Place both pans in the oven, then add very hot water to the bigger pan until it's within 1 inch (2.5 cm) of the top of the smaller pan.

Bake the bread pudding for 30 minutes. Remove the foil and bake for another 15 minutes, until the top is golden brown. Remove both pans from the oven, take the bread pudding out of the water bath and let it cool for 10 minutes while you make the chocolate sauce.

To make the chocolate sauce: Place the chocolate chips in a large heatproof bowl. Combine the milk, cream, brown sugar and salt in a medium saucepan over medium-high heat and bring them just to a boil. Immediately remove the saucepan from the heat and carefully pour the milk mixture over the chocolate chips. Let it sit for 1 minute, then whisk the sauce until it's smooth.

Serve the bread pudding warm with the chocolate sauce poured on top and extra cookies and cream ice cream on the side, if you'd like.

BREAD PUDDING

10 Mega Stuf Oreo cookies (or Double Stuf)

8–10 cups (240–300 g) cubed, somewhat stale challah bread or French bread

3 egg yolks

2 large eggs

⅛ tsp salt

1½ cups (360 ml) heavy cream

1½ cups (360 ml) melted cookies and cream ice cream

Cookies and cream ice cream (optional)

CHOCOLATE SAUCE

1½ cups (252 g) semisweet chocolate chips

1 cup (240 ml) whole milk

1 cup (240 ml) heavy cream

2 tbsp (28 g) packed brown sugar

⅛ tsp salt

NOTE: Use premium ice cream for this recipe; it has the higher butterfat content that you need for the custard.

BANANA SPLIT CREAM PIE

YIELD
Serves 6 to 8

When I was a kid, every ice cream parlor had a banana split on the menu. Every kid wanted one because it had *three* scoops of ice cream: one vanilla, one strawberry and one chocolate, with a banana cut in half lengthwise. The sauces varied from place to place, but were usually strawberry, hot fudge, caramel, pineapple or marshmallow, to name a few. Then came the whipped cream and chopped nuts, and of course a cherry on top. This cream pie is an ode to the ever-popular sundae, with a custard base made with banana liqueur and melted ice cream and then mixed with both strawberry and chocolate, to make sure you get all your favorite flavors of a banana split.

CRUST

1¾ cups (219 g) all-purpose flour

½ cup (50 g) crushed sugar or waffle cones

½ tsp salt

2 tbsp (25 g) granulated sugar

11 tbsp (150 g) unsalted butter, chilled and cut into ½-inch (13-mm) cubes

4–5 tbsp (60–75 ml) ice water

FILLING

¼ cup (60 ml) banana liqueur

1 (2¼-tsp [7-g]) packet powdered unflavored gelatin

4 egg yolks

¾ cup (150 g) granulated sugar

3 tbsp (24 g) cornstarch

2 cups (480 ml) whole milk

¾ cup (180 ml) melted vanilla ice cream

⅓ cup (108 g) strawberry jam

¼ cup (22 g) unsweetened cocoa powder

½ cup (84 g) semisweet chocolate chips

To make the crust: In the bowl of a stand mixer fitted with the whisk attachment, combine the flour, crushed cones, salt and sugar. Mix on low speed for about 30 seconds. Add the butter cubes to the flour mixture and combine on low speed for 1 to 1½ minutes, until the mixture looks crumbly. Add the ice water 1 tablespoon (15 ml) at a time, mixing on low speed for 10 seconds after each addition. After 4 tablespoons (60 ml), the dough should begin to clump together in a ball. If not, continue mixing about 10 more seconds. If it looks too dry, add another tablespoon (15 ml) of ice water.

Turn off the mixer and use your hands to gently mold the dough into a thick disk. Wrap it in plastic wrap and refrigerate for at least 1 hour.

Preheat the oven to 425°F (220°C).

Unwrap the dough and transfer it to a lightly floured work surface. Roll it into a ⅛-inch (3-mm)-thick circle large enough to line the bottom and sides of a 9-inch (23-cm) deep-dish pie pan. Wrap the dough lightly over the rolling pin and place it in the ungreased pie pan. Press it into place. Use a fork to prick the bottom of the crust.

Cover the bottom and sides of the crust with a sheet of parchment paper and fill the bottom with pie weights or dried beans. Bake for 10 minutes. Remove the weights and parchment paper. If the crust is not golden brown, return it to the oven for 1 to 3 minutes. Cool the crust on a rack and set it aside while you make the filling.

To make the filling: Pour the banana liqueur into a small metal bowl, sprinkle the gelatin on top and let it soften for 5 minutes.

Fill a small saucepan with 2 inches (5 cm) of water and bring it to a simmer. Set the bowl with the gelatin over the simmering water and warm the gelatin until it has completely dissolved and looks clear, about 3 to 5 minutes. No need to stir. Set aside.

(continued)

BANANA SPLIT CREAM PIE (CONTINUED)

In the bowl of a stand mixer with the whisk attachment, beat the egg yolks while gradually adding the sugar 1 tablespoon (15 g) at a time. Whisk until the mixture lightens to a pale yellow, about 10 minutes total. Add the cornstarch and beat until it's fully combined. Leave everything in the mixer while you do the next step.

In a medium saucepan over medium heat, heat the milk and vanilla ice cream until they begin to simmer. Take the pan off the heat and let it sit for 5 minutes.

Turn the mixer to medium, then gradually pour the hot milk and ice cream into the yolk mixture. When they're fully combined, pour the whole thing into a clean medium saucepan set over medium heat. Whisk constantly until the filling begins to thicken and coats the back of a spoon, about 3 to 5 minutes. Reduce the heat and whisk for 2 minutes more. Remove the pan from the heat and whisk in the gelatin mixture, being sure to incorporate it thoroughly.

Divide the filling evenly among three medium bowls. Leave one bowl alone. In another bowl, mix the strawberry jam into the filling. In the last bowl, add the cocoa powder and mix until it's fully combined. Let the fillings cool completely, about 30 minutes.

While you are waiting, put the chocolate in a small microwave-safe bowl and melt in the microwave on medium-high in 30-second bursts. Check after each burst to ensure the chocolate does not burn. Using a pastry brush or the back of a spoon, evenly coat the bottom and sides of the baked and cooled crust with the melted chocolate. Refrigerate the pie crust to let the chocolate harden and set, about 10 to 15 minutes.

To assemble the pie: Spoon the strawberry layer of custard into the bottom of the crust, followed by the plain layer and then the chocolate layer. Cover the pie with plastic wrap, making sure it touches the top of the custard. This is important because it prevents the custard from forming a skin—and no one wants skin on their custard. Place the pie in the fridge overnight.

To make the topping: Slice the bananas and place them in a large bowl with the lemon-lime soda (this helps prevent browning). Let them sit a minute or two, then remove the banana slices from the bowl and place them on a paper towel.

Remove the pie from the fridge and take off the plastic wrap. Arrange the banana slices on top of the pie. Put the cream and powdered sugar in a large bowl and whip until stiff peaks form, about 7 to 8 minutes. (Do this in a stand mixer or with a handheld electric beater.) Spoon the whipped cream onto the pie. Yes, I like a lot of whipped cream. Garnish with sprinkles and nuts and even a cherry or two.

TOPPING

2 ripe bananas

1 (12-oz [355-ml]) can lemon-lime soda

2 cups (480 ml) heavy cream

4 tsp (10 g) powdered sugar

Sprinkles, for garnish

Chopped nuts, for garnish

Maraschino cherries, for garnish

NOTE: Yes, this recipe uses banana liquor. The alcohol is cooked out as you heat the custard, so you can still serve it to kiddos.

MINT CHOCOLATE CHIP CUPCAKES

YIELD
Makes 20 to 22

My dad's birthday always meant two things: We were having German chocolate cake and we were having mint chocolate chip ice cream with it. In retrospect, mint and coconut really don't go together (though I have been known to eat a Samoa and a Thin Mint at the same time), but it's just what we did. To this day mint chocolate chip ice cream is still easily his favorite. So for Dad I made Mint Chocolate Chip Cupcakes baked with melted mint chocolate chip ice cream and topped with a mint buttercream. This recipe requires an extra step of dipping the cupcakes in a chocolate coating, but it makes for a great look—and it's pretty tasty, too.

For the mint chocolate chip cupcakes: Preheat the oven to 350°F (175°C). Spray two 12-cup muffin pans with nonstick baking spray.

In the bowl of a stand mixer with the paddle attachment, cream the butter until it's smooth, about 2 minutes. Add the sugar gradually and beat until the mixture is fluffy, about 3 minutes. Add the eggs one at a time, beating well after each addition.

In a medium bowl, mix together the flour, baking powder and salt. Add the dry ingredients to the butter and sugar in three parts, alternating with the melted ice cream and vanilla. With each addition, beat until the ingredients are incorporated but do not overbeat. Add a few drops of food coloring and beat until it's fully incorporated. Turn off the mixer, and using a rubber spatula, scrape down the batter in the bowl to make sure the ingredients are well blended. Fold in the chocolate chips.

Carefully spoon the batter into the muffin pans, filling each cup about three-quarters full. Bake for 20 to 25 minutes, or until a cake tester inserted in the center of a cupcake comes out clean. Cool the cupcakes in the tins for 15 minutes, then remove them and cool completely on a wire rack before frosting.

To make the buttercream: Fill a small saucepan with 2 inches (5 cm) of water and bring it to a simmer. Place the egg whites and sugar in the metal bowl of a stand mixer and set it over the simmering water (the bowl should not touch the water). Heat, stirring occasionally, until the mixture is 160°F (71°C) or hot to the touch, about 6 to 8 minutes. Leave the pan gently simmering.

Transfer the bowl to a stand mixer with the whisk attachment and beat on high speed until medium stiff peaks form, about 8 minutes. Reduce the speed to medium-low and add the butter one cube at a time, letting it incorporate into the meringue for a few moments before adding more. Add the peppermint extract, melted white chocolate and salt, and beat on high for 1 to 2 minutes until everything is smooth and creamy. Add some green food coloring and mix. Fold in the mini chocolate chips.

(continued)

MINT CHOCOLATE CHIP CUPCAKES

1 cup (227 g) unsalted butter, at room temperature

2 cups (400 g) granulated sugar

4 large eggs, at room temperature

2¾ cups (344 g) all-purpose flour

1½ tsp (7 g) baking powder

½ tsp salt

1 cup (240 ml) mint chocolate chip ice cream, melted

1 tsp vanilla extract

Green food coloring

1 cup (168 g) mini semisweet chocolate chips

MINT SWISS MERINGUE BUTTERCREAM

1 cup (240 ml) egg whites (about 9)

2 cups (400 g) granulated sugar

3 cups (681 g) unsalted butter, cubed, at room temperature

1 tbsp (15 ml) peppermint extract

10 oz (283 g) white chocolate, melted and cooled slightly

¼ tsp salt

Green food coloring

½ cup (86 g) mini semisweet chocolate chips

MINT CHOCOLATE CHIP CUPCAKES
(CONTINUED)

Frost the cupcakes however you like. If you are using a piping bag, make sure the tip size is big enough that the chocolate chips do not get stuck. Place the cupcakes in the fridge while you make the mint white chocolate coating.

To make the mint white chocolate coating: Combine the white chocolate and oil in a medium heatproof bowl and set it over your saucepan of barely simmering water. Stir until the chocolate is melted and smooth. Add the peppermint extract and food coloring and mix until everything is fully incorporated. Transfer the mixture to a small bowl and let it cool for about 15 minutes.

Set a wire rack on a large baking sheet. Holding each cupcake by its bottom, dip each frosted cupcake in the white chocolate coating to coat the frosting, allowing the excess to drip off. Transfer the cupcakes to the wire rack. Spoon more coating around the top edges of the cupcakes, so it drips down. Garnish the tops and sides of the cupcakes with some mini chocolate chips.

MINT WHITE CHOCOLATE COATING

12 oz (340 g) white chocolate, finely chopped

3 tbsp (45 ml) vegetable oil

½ tsp peppermint extract

Green food coloring

Mini semisweet chocolate chips, for garnish

ATLANTIC BEACH PIE THUMBPRINT COOKIES

YIELD
Makes about 24

I had never heard of Atlantic Beach pie in my life until I saw my favorite ice cream shop turn it into an ice cream flavor. After some quick Internet searching I learned that it's very similar to key lime pie, which is one of my all-time favorites. Instead of key lime, the pie is usually made with either all lemons or a combo of both lemons and limes (which I have chosen). In place of graham crackers for the crust, the pie contains crushed saltine crackers to give it a salty-sweet combo. I never did get to try the ice cream version, but I have made the pie several times and thought it would make a fun cookie.

To make the Atlantic Beach pie filling: Place the cream cheese in the bowl of a stand mixer fitted with the paddle attachment. Mix the cream cheese until it's smooth, about 2 minutes. Add the lemon and lime juices and the condensed milk and mix on low for 30 seconds. Increase the speed to medium and blend for 2 minutes. Scrape everything into a medium bowl, cover with plastic wrap and refrigerate for 2 hours or overnight.

To make the cookies: In the bowl of a stand mixer with the paddle attachment, cream the butter and sugar until they're light and fluffy, about 3 minutes. Add the egg, vanilla and salt, and beat on low speed until everything is fully combined. Add the flour and beat on low until it's fully incorporated. Wrap the dough in plastic wrap and refrigerate for 1 hour.

Preheat the oven to 350°F (175°C). Line two baking sheets with parchment paper.

Using a fork, beat together the egg white and water in a small bowl. Put the cracker crumbs in a separate bowl.

Remove the dough from the fridge and shape it into 1-inch (2.5-cm) balls. Dip the balls in the egg white, allowing the excess to drip off. Then roll them in the cracker crumbs to coat. Put the cookie balls on the prepared baking sheets, spacing them 2 inches (5 cm) apart. Using a 1-teaspoon measuring spoon or your thumb, make an indentation in the center of each cookie.

Bake the cookies, one sheet at a time, until the edges are set, 12 to 13 minutes. When I take them out of the oven, I like to press in my thumb or 1-teaspoon spoon again, to make the indentation really big in the cookie; it's easier to make while they are still warm. Transfer the cookies to a cooling rack.

When the cookies are cool, pipe or spoon the Atlantic Beach pie filling into the indentations. Keep them in an airtight container for up to 5 days in the fridge.

NOTES: You will need to make the filling at least 1 hour ahead of the cookies. Both the filling and the dough need to be chilled, but the filling takes longer. I often just make the filling the night before.

ATLANTIC BEACH PIE FILLING

8 oz (225 g) cream cheese, at room temperature

6 tbsp (90 ml) fresh lemon juice

4 tbsp (60 ml) fresh lime juice

1¼ cups (300 ml) sweetened condensed milk

COOKIES

½ cup (114 g) unsalted butter, at room temperature

⅔ cup (132 g) granulated sugar

1 large egg

½ tsp vanilla extract

¼ tsp salt

1⅓ cups (166 g) all-purpose flour

1 egg white

1 tsp water

1 cup (84 g) finely crushed saltine crackers

1½–2 cups (360–480 ml) Atlantic Beach pie filling

ROCKY ROAD BROWNIE PIE

YIELD
Serves 8

Rocky Road was the first ice cream I loved that was chocolate-based. Normally I am not a chocolate girl, but there was just something about rocky road that I loved. I think probably the mini marshmallows. I'm a sucker for those. This is an intensely rich and dense brown pie, and you definitely need a giant scoop of ice cream or two (I won't judge) to go with it!

1 bottom pie crust (recipe of your choice or store-bought)

1 (14-oz [397-g]) can sweetened condensed milk

¼ cup (57 g) unsalted butter, cut into 8 pieces

½ cup (44 g) unsweetened cocoa powder

3 large eggs

3 tbsp (24 g) all-purpose flour

1 tsp vanilla extract

¾ cup (126 g) milk chocolate chips

½ cup (59 g) chopped walnuts

½ cup (20 g) Mallow Bits

Ice cream (optional)

Preheat the oven to 350°F (175°C). Grease a 9-inch (23-cm) pie pan. Roll out the crust and place it in the pan.

In a medium saucepan over low heat, combine the condensed milk, butter and cocoa powder. Stir occasionally so the mixture does not stick to the pan and scorch. Remove from the heat when all the ingredients are melted and fully combined, about 3 minutes.

In a large bowl, lightly beat the eggs. Add a small amount of the hot chocolate mixture, a couple of spoonfuls at a time, to the egg mixture, whisking the whole time. Do this three times to temper the eggs. Then stir the remaining chocolate mixture into the eggs, whisking until they're fully combined. Add the flour and vanilla to the mixture, and mix with a wooden spoon until all the ingredients are incorporated.

Spread half the chocolate chips, walnuts and Mallow Bits over the bottom of the pie crust. Pour the chocolate batter into the pie shell. Top with the remaining chocolate chips, walnuts and Mallow Bits. Bake for 40 minutes.

Cool, and serve with ice cream if you'd like.

NOTE: Mallow Bits and mini marshmallows are not the same thing. Mallow Bits are more like the marshmallow bits you find in prepackaged cocoa mix. Mini marshmallows will not work, as they will melt into the mixture and disappear, creating a gluey texture that you do not want. You can find Mallow Bits in the baking section of grocery stores and large chains like Walmart and Target.

CHUBBY HUBBY FUDGE

YIELD
Makes about 24 pieces

This fudge is my love letter to chubby hubby ice cream. I don't like to limit myself to having one favorite ice cream flavor, but chubby hubby is definitely up in my top five. If you are not familiar with the flavor, it's been described as "vanilla malt ice cream with peanutty fudge-covered pretzels with fudge and peanut butter swirls." I changed it up a little by making a vanilla and peanut butter malted fudge with chocolate and pretzels, but once it's in your mouth the overall flavor is the same.

2 cups (384 g) superfine granulated sugar

½ cup (114 g) unsalted butter, cut into 8 pieces

½ cup (120 ml) heavy cream

1 cup (168 g) finely chopped white chocolate

1 cup (168 g) peanut butter chips

1 (7-oz [198-g]) jar marshmallow creme

½ tsp vanilla extract

2 tbsp (15 g) malted milk powder

¼ cup (22 g) powdered peanut butter

¾ cup (126 g) roughly chopped semi-sweet chocolate

1 cup (115 g) crushed pretzels

Line an 8 x 8-inch (20 x 20-cm) pan with parchment paper, with enough of an overhang that you can lift the fudge out later. Coat the paper with a thin layer of nonstick baking spray.

In a large, heavy-bottomed saucepan, combine the sugar, butter and cream, and stir the ingredients until they're just combined. Bring to a boil over medium heat, then reduce the heat to a hair above medium-low and cook for 7 to 10 minutes, stirring constantly, until your thermometer reads 234°F (112°C), the soft ball stage.

When you reach the right temperature, remove the pan from the heat and add the white chocolate and the peanut butter chips, stirring vigorously with a wooden spoon until the chocolate and peanut butter chips have melted and the mixture is smooth. Add the marshmallow creme, vanilla, malted milk powder and powdered peanut butter, and mix until everything is well blended. At this stage the fudge can sometimes seem a little watery. You need to keep stirring and stirring until it almost feels like your arm might fall off, and it will come together.

Fold in the chopped chocolate pieces and crushed pretzels, trying to get them evenly distributed as best you can. You want to see chocolate streaks in the fudge. Pour the fudge into the prepared pan and top with more chocolate pieces and pretzel pieces, if desired.

Let the fudge cool to room temperature and then lift it out of the pan by the edges of the parchment paper. Place it on a cutting board and cut into whatever number of squares you want. I usually go for 24.

NOTES: You can make your own superfine sugar by running granulated sugar in a dry blender or a food processor. Pulse a few times to make the sugar grains smaller, but be careful not to blend it too fine or you will end up with powdered sugar. I make it in large batches and just have it in a container that says "candy sugar," because I use it for making both fudge and caramel. Using the superfine sugar helps make a less grainy fudge.

You can find powdered peanut butter at most grocery stores. It's sometimes in the health food section.

CEREAL
KILLERS

RECIPES INSPIRED BY
MY FAVORITE SUGARY CEREALS

I originally discovered the joy of adding cereal milk to baked goods out of a combo of necessity and laziness. I was thirteen and very much in full teenage angst mode, wanting to be independent and prove I could do things on my own. I started to make a cake but realized halfway through the recipe that I had used the last of the milk on the Count Chocula cereal I had just eaten. Which, luckily, thanks to my lazy teen ways, was still sitting in the bowl on the counter. So I measured the milk out, threw it in the batter and hoped for the best. I'm not totally sure what the cake was supposed to taste like, but I loved how it turned out.

With that I was hooked on making things with cereal and cereal milk. Sometimes it worked and sometimes it didn't. But it was always fun trying.

There was the very horrid Lucky Charms rum daiquiri that my poor dad was subjected to during my mixology phase in my teen years. Yes, teens. For some reason my parents let me make cocktails at age thirteen. You can read more about that in the chapter It's Five O'Clock Somewhere (page 120).

In college, our cafeteria had giant dispensers of sugary cereal that would easily make anyone and everyone gain the Freshman Fifteen. But as I do with most foods, I found a way to make it have even more calories. I would sneak cereal back to the dorm, infuse it in cream and make caramel sauce. But wait, there's more! I would take the caramel sauce with me to the cafeteria, where I would layer cereal with soft-serve ice cream and top it all with my caramel sauce. While not everyone got to have the caramel sauce, I did start the trend of students making cereal sundaes—helping to solidify the Freshman Thirty.

I've used cereal milk in almost anything that can be made with regular milk or cream. It makes great ice cream and great pastry cream, both of which you will see here in this chapter. My hope is that if you have never used cereal in your baking, you will try these recipes and be inspired to do some experimenting of your own.

CAP'N CRUNCH BOSTON CREAM PIE LAYER CAKE

YIELD
Serves 8 to 10

Now you can have all of the flavor of Cap'n Crunch cereal without losing the roof of your mouth. Custard is one of the great ways of incorporating cereal into baked goods. Here I have taken the traditional Boston cream pie and added Cap'n Crunch to both the cake batter and the custard, and turned it into a 6-inch (15-cm) layer cake. I find this size produces a moister cake. If you are, however, a traditionalist, I do list the bake time for a 9-inch (23-cm) cake.

To make the Cap'n Crunch milk and cream: The day before you're making the cake, mix the milk with 2 cups (72 g) of Cap'n Crunch cereal in an airtight container. Mix the cream and the remaining 1 cup (36 g) of Cap'n Crunch cereal in another airtight container. Put both in the fridge for 8 hours or overnight. Then strain out the cereal.

To make the custard filling: In a medium bowl, whisk together the yolks, sugar and cornstarch until they are completely combined. Set aside.

In a medium saucepan over medium-low heat, bring the Cap'n Crunch milk to a gentle boil (think tiny bubbles at the surface with just a few larger bubbles). Remove the pan from the heat and slowly whisk about ⅓ cup (80 ml) of the hot milk into the yolk mixture to temper the eggs and keep them from scrambling.

Then pour the yolk and milk mixture into the saucepan and place it over medium-high heat. Bring to a full boil, whisking constantly, for 1 to 2 minutes. Watch this carefully, as it can go from a liquid to custard consistency rather quickly. Remove the pan from the heat as soon as you have custard. Scrape the bottom of the pan with a spatula and whisk the custard until it's smooth. Whisk in the butter until it's melted.

Immediately strain the custard through a fine-mesh sieve into a medium bowl, to ensure you didn't get any scrambled egg action. Whisk in the vanilla extract. Cover the surface of the custard with plastic wrap or else you will get a skin . . . and you don't want custard skin. Let it cool to room temperature, then refrigerate for 2 hours, or until the custard is well chilled. I usually make the custard the night before.

Just before assembling the cake, transfer the custard to the bowl of an electric mixer with the whisk attachment. Add the cream and beat at high speed until it is light and forms soft peaks, about 1 minute.

To make the sponge cake: Preheat the oven to 350°F (175°C). Position a rack in the center of the oven. Line two 6-inch (15-cm) cake pans (or one 9-inch [23-cm] cake pan if you're going traditional) with parchment paper circles and spray the bottoms and sides with nonstick baking spray.

CAP'N CRUNCH MILK AND CREAM

2 cups (480 ml) whole milk

3 cups (108 g) Cap'n Crunch cereal, divided

1 cup (240 ml) heavy cream

CUSTARD FILLING

3 egg yolks

¼ cup (50 g) granulated sugar

2 tbsp (15 g) cornstarch

1 cup (240 ml) Cap'n Crunch milk

1 tbsp (14 g) unsalted butter

1 tsp vanilla extract

½ cup (120 ml) heavy cream

SPONGE CAKE

1½ cups (180 g) cake flour

1¼ tsp (6 g) baking powder

¼ tsp salt

½ cup (120 ml) Cap'n Crunch milk

¼ cup (57 g) unsalted butter, cut into 4 pieces

3 large eggs, at room temperature

¾ cup (150 g) granulated sugar

1 tsp vanilla extract

(continued)

CAP'N CRUNCH BOSTON CREAM PIE LAYER CAKE (CONTINUED)

In a medium bowl, sift together the cake flour, baking powder and salt. (Yes, you really have to sift.) Set aside.

In a small saucepan, combine the Cap'n Crunch milk and butter and heat over medium heat just until the butter is melted. Remove the pan from the heat and set aside.

In the bowl of a stand mixer with the whisk attachment, beat the eggs at high speed until they're blended, about 1 minute. Gradually add the sugar and vanilla and beat until the mixture is pale and has tripled in volume, about 5 minutes. Turn off the mixer. Sift (yes, again) one-third of the flour mixture over the egg mixture and gently fold it in with a rubber spatula. Repeat with the remaining flour mixture in two more additions.

Reheat the milk and butter mixture to just under a boil. Add it all at once to the eggs and flour, and gently fold it in. Scrape the batter into the prepared pans.

Bake for 30 to 35 minutes for two 6-inch (15-cm) cakes or 20 to 25 minutes for one 9-inch (23-cm) cake, until they spring back when lightly touched and a cake tester inserted into the center comes out clean. Cool the cakes in the pans on a wire rack for 10 minutes. Then run a knife around the edges of the pans and invert the cakes onto the wire rack. Flip the cakes so they are right side up.

To make the chocolate glaze: In a small saucepan, bring the Cap'n Crunch cream to a boil over medium-high heat. Remove from the heat and add the chocolate to the pan. Stir until the chocolate is completely melted and the glaze is smooth. Stir in the vanilla. The glaze should be nice and shiny. Transfer the glaze to a small bowl. Cover the surface of the glaze with a piece of plastic wrap and let it cool for about 10 minutes before using.

To assemble the cake: Using a long serrated knife, cut the cakes horizontally in half to make four layers if you're making a 6-inch (15-cm) cake or two layers if you're making a 9-inch (23-cm) cake.

Save one of the smooth bottom layers for the top of the cake. Place the other bottom cake layer cut side up on a serving plate. Scrape one-third of the custard filling onto the layer and, using a small offset metal spatula or a knife, spread it into an even layer. Add the next layer of cake, followed by another one-third of the custard. Add the third layer of cake and spread it with the remaining custard. Top with the fourth cake layer, cut side down. (If you're making a 9-inch [23-cm] cake, simply spread all the custard between the two cake layers.)

Pour the warm glaze over the top of the cake, allowing some of it to drizzle down the sides. Serve the cake immediately, or store it in the refrigerator in a covered container for up to 1 day. Bring the cake to room temperature before serving.

CHOCOLATE GLAZE

½ cup (120 ml) Cap'n Crunch cream

3 oz (85 g) semisweet chocolate, finely chopped

½ tsp vanilla extract

NOTES: The 6-inch (15-cm) cake does not have one thick layer of custard, like a traditional Boston cream pie. This is by design. Every time I make a cake with the traditional single layer of custard, the minute I slice the cake or cut it to take a bite, the custard squeezes out the sides.

The cereal soaks up a lot of liquid, but if you have any leftover from the Cap'n Crunch milk or cream, try it in your coffee.

OOPS! ALL BERRIES TRES LECHES CAKE

YIELD
Serves 16 to 20

Tres leches is an odd cake. There, I said it. It starts with a super dry sponge cake that gets soaked in three different types of milk (hence the name tres leches). The milk mixture gives it an almost custard-like texture, which makes for a silky cake. To which I have added a variety of Cap'n Crunch called Oops! All Berries. I'll admit that while I am happy Cap'n Crunch now makes a cereal with nothing but Crunch Berries, the name of it does nothing for me. I always picture Cap'n Crunch in a Brittany Spears–type video singing. For real, that happened in a dream. Twice. And yes, it's a sad life when that's what I am dreaming about. He was at least dressed in the dream—thank God. Nonetheless, dumb name or not, it makes for a yummy cereal that my husband and I snack on regularly. And it works well in this cake.

For the Oops! All Berries milk and cream: The day before you're making the cake, combine the milk with ½ cup (16 g) of Oops! All Berries cereal in an airtight container. Combine the cream with the remaining 1½ cups (48 g) of Oops! All Berries cereal in another airtight container. Refrigerate both containers for 8 hours or overnight. Then strain out the cereal.

To make the cake: Preheat the oven to 350°F (175°C). Generously spray a 9 x 13–inch (23 x 33–cm) pan with nonstick baking spray.

In a large bowl, combine the flour, baking powder and salt. Set aside.

Put the egg whites aside. In the bowl of a stand mixer with the whisk attachment, beat the egg yolks with ¾ cup (150 g) of sugar on high speed until the yolks are pale yellow. Stir in the Oops! All Berries milk and the vanilla. Pour the egg yolk mixture over the flour mixture and stir very gently until it's combined.

In another bowl of a stand mixer with the whisk attachment, beat the egg whites on high speed until soft peaks form, about 2 minutes. With the mixer still on, pour in the remaining ¼ cup (50 g) of sugar and beat until the egg whites are stiff but not dry, about 3 minutes. Fold the egg white mixture into the batter very gently, until it's just combined.

Pour the batter into the prepared pan and spread the top with a spatula to even out the surface. Bake for 35 to 45 minutes, or until a toothpick inserted into the center comes out clean. Turn the cake out onto a rimmed platter (if it doesn't have a rim you will lose the milk mixture when you pour it over the cake) and let it cool.

(continued)

OOPS! ALL BERRIES MILK AND CREAM

½ cup (120 ml) whole milk

2 cups (64 g) Cap'n Crunch Oops! All Berries cereal, divided, plus more for garnish

2 cups (480 ml) heavy cream

CAKE

1 cup (125 g) all-purpose flour

1½ tsp (7 g) baking powder

¼ tsp salt

5 large eggs, separated

1 cup (200 g) granulated sugar, divided

⅓ cup (80 ml) Oops! All Berries milk

1 tsp vanilla bean paste

1 (12-oz [354-ml]) can evaporated milk

1 (14-oz [397-g]) can sweetened condensed milk

¼ cup (60 ml) Oops! All Berries cream

OOPS! ALL BERRIES TRES LECHES CAKE (CONTINUED)

When the cake is cool, combine the evaporated milk, condensed milk and Oops! All Berries cream in a small pitcher. Pierce the surface of the cake with a fork several times. Slowly drizzle some of the milk and cream mixture over the cake. Wait until the cake absorbs the liquid before adding more. Sometimes it takes all of the milk mixture and sometimes it is saturated when you still have about 1 cup (240 ml) of the milk mixture left over. It just depends. Let the cake sit to absorb the milk mixture for 30 minutes.

To make the whipped cream frosting: Combine the cream and the Oops! All Berries cream in the bowl of a stand mixer fitted with the whisk attachment. Whip until the cream is thick and spreadable, about 2 minutes. Use an offset spatula to spread it over the surface of the cake. Decorate the cake with more Oops! All Berries cereal.

NOTES: Depending on what mixture of Oops! All Berries cereal you get (green vs. purple) your milk and cream may take on a very unpleasant color. I tend to add more purple and blue berries to the mix so that mine is more purple-y. However, feel free to use food coloring to color the milk and cream if you get a strange color.

This recipe works well for a variety of cereals. Any fruity cereal can work. Honey-flavored cereals would also be good. Heck, even chocolate cereals would work well. Maybe just stay away from the high-fiber cereals for this recipe.

WHIPPED CREAM FROSTING

1 cup (240 ml) heavy cream

1 cup (240 ml) Oops! All Berries cream

FUDGE-FROSTED CINNAMON TOAST CRUNCH HOT MILK CAKE

YIELD
Serves 8 to 10

I really didn't get into eating Cinnamon Toast Crunch until I was an adult, but it's now one of my go-to nighttime snacks. It's comforting to me: Any time I was sick when I was growing up my mom would feed me cinnamon toast and lemon-lime soda. How this helped I don't know, but to this day if I'm sick that is what I crave. This is a single-layer cake with an old-fashioned fudge frosting that I got from my aunt's grandmother (on her side). I only met her grandmother once and only had that frosting once, but it was memorable enough that I bugged my aunt until I got the recipe for it . . . at age ten.

To make the Cinnamon Toast Crunch milk: The day before you're making the cake, mix the milk with the Cinnamon Toast Crunch cereal in an airtight container. Put it in the fridge for 8 hours or overnight. Then strain out the cereal.

To make the cake: Preheat the oven to 325°F (160°C). Line a 9-inch (23-cm) round cake pan with a parchment paper circle and spray with nonstick baking spray.

In the bowl of a stand mixer with the paddle attachment, beat together the eggs and sugar until they're very thick and pale, about 3 to 5 minutes. Beat in the vanilla for 30 seconds. While you're beating the eggs and sugar, heat the Cinnamon Toast Crunch milk and butter in a small saucepan over medium-low heat just to a simmer, about 3 minutes. Add the hot Cinnamon Toast Crunch milk to the egg mixture in a slow, steady stream as you continue beating.

In a separate medium bowl, whisk together the flour, baking powder, cinnamon and salt. Remove the bowl from the mixer and, using a spatula, fold the dry ingredients into the wet ingredients, stirring until they're just combined. Pour the batter into the prepared cake pan.

Bake for 50 minutes, or until the cake is a deep golden brown and starts to pull away from the sides of the pan. Remove the cake from the oven and cool it in the pan for 10 to 15 minutes. Then run a knife around the sides of the pan. Flip the cake out onto a wire rack to fully cool while you prepare the frosting.

To make the fudge frosting: In the bowl of a stand mixer with the paddle attachment, cream the butter and 2 cups (240 g) of powdered sugar until they're fully combined. Add the melted chocolate, cinnamon and cocoa powder, and beat on low speed until everything is fully incorporated. Add the remaining 2 cups (240 g) of sugar and the Cinnamon Toast Crunch milk. If the frosting is still too thick, add a little more of the milk. If it's too thin, add a little more powdered sugar.

Frost the top and sides of the cake. Top with extra Cinnamon Toast Crunch.

CINNAMON TOAST CRUNCH MILK

1½ cups (360 ml) whole milk

1 cup (41 g) Cinnamon Toast Crunch cereal

CAKE

3 large eggs

1½ cups (300 g) granulated sugar

1 tsp vanilla extract

¾ cup (180 ml) Cinnamon Toast Crunch milk

1 tbsp (14 g) unsalted butter

1½ cups (188 g) all-purpose flour

1½ tsp (7 g) baking powder

½ tsp ground cinnamon

½ tsp salt

FUDGE FROSTING

2 cups (454 g) unsalted butter, at room temperature

4 cups (480 g) powdered sugar, divided

2 cups (336 g) semisweet chocolate chips, melted and slightly cooled

½ tsp ground cinnamon

2 tbsp (11 g) unsweetened cocoa powder

2 tbsp (30 ml) Cinnamon Toast Crunch milk

Cinnamon Toast Crunch cereal, for garnish

FROSTED FLAKES BANANA CHOCOLATE CHIP POUND CAKE

YIELD
Serves 8

Frosted Flakes have been around since the 1950s, and while not the first sugary cereal on the market, it was pretty close. And they had a slogan that stuck. I mean, who doesn't know that they're grrrrreat? They are more than great in this banana-based pound cake, filled with Frosted Flakes and milk chocolate pieces all topped with more chocolate. If you haven't been coating your loaf cakes in chocolate, you have been missing out!

To make the cake: Preheat the oven to 350°F (175°C). Spray a 9 x 5 x 3–inch (23 x 13 x 8–cm) loaf pan with nonstick baking spray.

Sift the flour, baking powder, baking soda and salt into a medium bowl and set aside. Combine the sour cream and mascarpone cheese in a small bowl and set aside.

In the bowl of a stand mixer fitted with the paddle attachment, beat the butter on high speed until it's soft and creamy, about 1 minute. Slowly add the sugar, 1 tablespoon (15 g) at a time, beating continuously on high speed. It should take 5 to 10 minutes to add all the sugar. I know that seems excessive, but it really does help with the texture of the cake. The mixture should be light, fluffy and creamy white. Stop the mixer and scrape down the sides of the bowl with a rubber spatula.

Turn the mixer on low speed. Add the eggs, one at a time. Be sure the first egg is completely incorporated and scrape down the sides of the bowl before adding the second one. Then add one-third of the flour mixture to the batter and beat until it is just incorporated. Add one-third of the mascarpone cheese mixture and beat until it is just incorporated. Add the flour and mascarpone mixture in two more additions, mixing until each addition is fully incorporated before adding the next.

Fold in the bananas, chocolate and Frosted Flakes. Pour the batter into the prepared loaf pan and bake for 1 hour and 15 minutes. Cool in the pan on a rack for 5 to 10 minutes, then remove the cake from the pan and set it on the rack to cool.

To make the chocolate coating: Put about 2 inches (5 cm) of water in a small saucepan and heat it over medium heat until it is hot but not boiling. Turn off the heat. Place the chocolate and butter in a small stainless steel bowl over the pot. Let them melt without stirring. When the chocolate and butter are just melted, whisk them together.

Use an offset spatula to frost the cake with the chocolate coating. Work fast, as it will harden up—which it is supposed to do. Add additional Frosted Flakes while the coating is still wet, if desired. Serve the cake at room temperature.

CAKE

2¼ cups (281 g) all-purpose flour

1 tbsp (14 g) baking powder

1 tsp baking soda

¼ tsp salt

½ cup (120 ml) sour cream

½ cup (116 g) mascarpone cheese (or cream cheese)

¾ cup (170 g) unsalted butter, at room temperature

1 cup (200 g) granulated sugar

2 large eggs

2 fully ripe bananas, puréed

1 cup (168 g) chopped milk chocolate

1 cup (42 g) Frosted Flakes cereal

CHOCOLATE COATING

¾ cup (170 g) finely chopped milk chocolate

4 tbsp (56 g) unsalted butter

Frosted Flakes, for garnish

HONEY BUNCHES OF OATS BAKLAVA CRÈME BRÛLÉE

YIELD
Makes 18

I made the original version of this dessert back when I was catering and a bride wanted both crème brûlée and baklava at her wedding . . . but only wanted one dessert. Ummm, okay. The result ended up being the hit of the wedding. While the original did not use cereal—just nuts—Honey Bunches of Oats goes perfectly with the dessert and adds a fun element. It's not a complicated recipe; all the steps just take some time.

To make the phyllo cups: Preheat the oven to 350°F (175°C). Spray one and a half 12-cup muffin pans with nonstick baking spray. (You will be using 18 of the cups.)

Combine the sugar and cinnamon in a small bowl and keep the cinnamon sugar handy. Cut all the phyllo dough into 6 x 6–inch (15 x 15–cm) squares. Keep the dough you are not working with wrapped up in plastic wrap or it will dry out. Lay one square on a flat surface, brush it with butter and sprinkle on about ½ teaspoon of the cinnamon sugar. Put another square on top of it and repeat three times, so you have four layers of dough with butter and cinnamon sugar between the layers. Push the dough stack into a cup in the muffin pan and use your hands to push it down the sides to form a cup. You will have overhang. Repeat until you have 18 muffin cups, each made from four layers of phyllo brushed with butter and sprinkled with cinnamon sugar.

Bake for 10 to 11 minutes. Let them cool for 1 minute, then remove the cups from the muffin pans. Store in a dry place. I usually make these a day before.

To make the crème brûlée: Preheat the oven to 325°F (160°C). Place an ungreased 9 x 13–inch (23 x 33–cm) baking dish in another baking pan big enough to hold it without touching the sides.

In a large saucepan, heat the cream and milk over medium heat until bubbles form around the sides of the pan. Quickly remove the pan from the heat. In a medium bowl, whisk together the egg yolks, sugar, honey and salt until they're blended but not foamy. Slowly stir in the hot cream mixture, whisking all the time.

Pour the whole thing into the smaller baking dish. Place both pans in the oven, then add very hot water to the bigger pan until it's within 1 inch (2.5 cm) of the top of the smaller pan. Bake until the center is just set and the top appears dull, 35 to 40 minutes. Immediately remove the dish from the water bath to a wire rack. Cool for 1 hour, then refrigerate until it's cold.

To make the baklava filling: In a medium bowl combine the cereal, almonds and honey, and mix well.

To assemble everything, scoop the crème brûlée into a piping bag (or you can spoon it). Pipe or spoon one layer of crème brûlée into the phyllo cup, then add a heaping spoonful or two of baklava filling, more crème brûlée, and then top with another spoonful or two of baklava filling. Drizzle a little honey over the top, if desired.

PHYLLO CUPS

1 cup (200 g) granulated sugar

1 tbsp (8 g) ground cinnamon

18 sheets phyllo dough (about 1 package)

1 cup (227 g) unsalted butter, melted

CRÈME BRÛLÉE

2½ cups (600 ml) heavy cream

½ cup (120 ml) whole milk

8 egg yolks, at room temperature

½ cup (100 g) granulated sugar

3 tbsp (45 ml) honey

¼ tsp salt

BAKLAVA FILLING

¾ cup (32 g) Honey Bunches of Oats cereal

½ cup (54 g) slivered almonds, chopped

½ cup (120 ml) honey, heated slightly, plus more for garnish

CAP'N CRUNCH PEANUT BUTTER NO-BAKE CHEESECAKE

YIELD
Serves about 8

My blog is more than fifteen years old. Back when I started, food blogging was not as big a thing as it is nowadays. Because of that, mine actually inspired many current bloggers to start their own blogs, which is very cool. One of those bloggers is my blogging BFF and partner in crime Kita, who runs Pass the Sushi and Girl Carnivore. One of the first recipes Kita loved of mine that she shared on her blog was an ice cream made with Cap'n Crunch cereal and peanut butter. In retrospect, I should have just used Cap'n Crunch Peanut Butter Crunch. This cheesecake is based on that flavor combo. I made it extra special by making a crust out of the cereal (think Rice Krispies treats), then filled it with a no-bake peanut butter cheesecake. This dessert is almost two desserts in one: cereal treats and cheesecake. I like to eat the no-bake cheesecake first and then finish off by eating the crust . . . but that's just me.

To make the Cap'n Crunch Peanut Butter cream: The day before you're making the cake, mix the cream with the Cap'n Crunch Peanut Butter cereal in an airtight container. Put it in the fridge for 8 hours or overnight. Then strain out the cereal.

To make the crust: Spray a 10-inch (25-cm) springform pan with nonstick baking spray.

Melt the butter over low heat in a large heavy-bottomed pot—the bigger the better, as the cereal will spill out if the pot is too small. Add the marshmallows to the melted butter and stir. Wait for them to melt almost completely, so you can see only a couple of intact marshmallows. This may take about 5 to 7 minutes. Remove the pot from the heat and add the vanilla. Mix until it's incorporated. Add the cereal and mix and mix and mix until the cereal is well coated. Make sure to stir up all the marshmallow at the bottom of the pot—it likes to hide there.

Using a spoon at first and then your clean hands, form the Cap'n Crunch Peanut Butter mixture into a crust in the springform pan, starting with the bottom and going all the way up the sides. If you crush some of the cereal, that is totally fine because the marshmallow will keep it together. You might have a little leftover that doesn't fit into the pan . . . just eat it.

To make the cheesecake: In the bowl of a stand mixer fitted with the whisk attachment, whip the cold Cap'n Crunch Peanut Butter cream into stiff peaks on medium-high speed, about 4 to 5 minutes. Set aside.

(continued)

CAP'N CRUNCH PEANUT BUTTER CREAM

2¼ cups (540 ml) heavy cream

1½ cups (54 g) Cap'n Crunch Peanut Butter Crunch cereal

CRUST

3 tbsp (42 g) unsalted butter

6 cups (300 g) mini marshmallows

½ tsp vanilla extract

7–8 cups (252–288 g) Cap'n Crunch Peanut Butter Crunch cereal

CHEESECAKE

1¾ cups (420 ml) Cap'n Crunch Peanut Butter cream, chilled

1 lb (450 g) cream cheese, at room temperature

½ cup (60 g) powdered sugar

¼ cup (60 ml) sour cream

½ cup (44 g) powdered peanut butter

½ cup (65 g) malted milk powder

1 tsp vanilla extract

CAP'N CRUNCH PEANUT BUTTER
NO-BAKE CHEESECAKE (CONTINUED)

In another bowl for the stand mixer fitted with the paddle attachment, beat the cream cheese and powdered sugar together on medium speed until the mixture is perfectly smooth and creamy, about 3 minutes. Scrape down the sides and across the bottom of the bowl with a rubber spatula as needed. Add the sour cream, powdered peanut butter, malted milk powder and vanilla. Beat for 2 to 3 minutes on medium-high speed until everything is smooth and combined. Make sure there are no large lumps of cream cheese. If there are lumps, keep beating until it's smooth.

Using a rubber spatula, fold the whipped Cap'n Crunch Peanut Butter cream into the cheesecake filling until it's combined. Do this as slowly as possible so you do not deflate the whipped cream. Pour the filling into the prepared crust and use an offset spatula to smooth the top.

Cover the cake tightly with plastic wrap or aluminum foil and refrigerate for at least 6 to 8 hours and up to 2 days. I like to chill mine overnight, as the longer it is in the fridge the better it sets.

Use a knife to loosen the chilled cheesecake from the rim of the springform pan, then remove the rim. Using a clean, sharp knife, cut the cake into slices. For neat slices, wipe the knife clean between each slice.

NOTES: This is not a normal crust; it is thicker than most and of course has marshmallows in it—which means it is sturdier than your normal crust.

Top it all with whipped cream and chocolate sauce from the store, if you'd like. Or make some of your own.

FRUITY PEBBLES CRUMB CAKE

YIELD
Makes 6 mini loaves

I love crumb-topped anything. I top cake, cinnamon rolls, muffins, pies, blondies, cookies, you name it, with crumb topping. If it goes in the oven, there is a good chance I've probably thrown crumb topping on it at one time. Fruity Pebbles form the crumbs here. I was more of a Froot Loops kid growing up, which makes no sense because I liked the Flintstones way more than toucans. Perhaps because I was already getting the Flintstones in vitamin form (purple Dino all the way), my mother felt I didn't need them in cereal form. But now that I'm the one doing the shopping, I get my vitamins in gummy form and my fruity cereal in pebble form. I prefer to make these as mini loaves because I feel baking is for sharing, but you can also make this recipe as two standard loaves. I'll give you bake times for both.

To make the Fruity Pebbles milk: The day before you're making the cake, mix the milk with the Fruity Pebbles cereal in an airtight container. Put it in the fridge for 8 hours or overnight. Then strain out the cereal.

To make the crumb topping: Put the sugar and salt in a medium bowl and mix until they're combined. Add the melted butter, Fruity Pebbles and the cake flour, and mix (hands work best for this). Squeeze the crumbs into large chunks and then break them up into smaller pieces. Set aside.

For the cake: Preheat the oven to 325°F (160°C). Spray six mini loaf pans or two standard loaf pans with nonstick baking spray.

In the bowl of a stand mixer with the paddle attachment, cream together the butter and sugar until they're fluffy and light yellow, about 3 minutes.

In another medium bowl, add the eggs, Fruity Pebbles milk, sour cream and vanilla and whisk until they're fully combined. In yet another medium bowl, combine the flour, baking powder, baking soda and salt.

Add one-third of the dry ingredients to the creamed butter mixture and mix on low until they're incorporated. Then, mixing on low between each addition, add half the wet mixture, then one-third of the dry mixture, then the rest of the wet, and finish with the rest of the dry until everything is fully combined, being careful to not over-mix. Remove the bowl from the mixer. Using a spatula, fold the Fruity Pebbles into the batter. Do your best to evenly distribute the cereal throughout the batter.

(continued)

FRUITY PEBBLES MILK

2 cups (480 ml) whole milk

1 cup (36 g) Fruity Pebbles cereal

CRUMB TOPPING

⅔ cup (132 g) granulated sugar

¼ tsp salt

½ cup (114 g) unsalted butter, melted and slightly cooled

⅓ cup (12 g) Fruity Pebbles cereal

1½ cups (180 g) cake flour

CAKE

½ cup (114 g) unsalted butter, at room temperature

1 cup (200 g) granulated sugar

2 large eggs

1 cup (240 ml) Fruity Pebbles milk

1 cup (240 ml) sour cream

1 tsp vanilla extract

2½ cups (300 g) cake flour

2 tsp (9 g) baking powder

½ tsp baking soda

Pinch of salt

1 cup (36 g) Fruity Pebbles cereal, plus more for garnish

FRUITY PEBBLES CRUMB CAKE (CONTINUED)

Using a regular-sized ice cream scoop, evenly distribute the batter among the six pans (or two). Break up the crumb topping as best you can, and evenly divide it over the top of each pan. The reality is that it's not going to be equal, but make it work. Bake for 30 to 35 minutes for mini loaves or 45 to 50 minutes for the standard loaves. When the cakes are done, a wooden skewer or knife inserted into the center should come out clean. Let them cool for 5 minutes in the pan, then remove them to a wire rack to cool while you make the glaze.

For the glaze: Simply whisk together the Fruity Pebbles milk, vanilla, butter and powdered sugar in a medium bowl. When the cakes are cool, pour the glaze over the tops. Top with some Fruity Pebbles cereal and press down a little on the cereal to help it adhere to the crumb topping. Let the glaze firm up, which should take about 1 hour, before you slice the cake.

GLAZE

6 tbsp (90 ml) Fruity Pebbles milk

1 tsp vanilla extract

2 tbsp (28 g) unsalted butter, melted

1½ cups (180 g) powdered sugar

NOTES: I glaze all of my crumb-topped baked goods because I find that when I don't glaze them a good chunk of the crumb tends to fall off. When you glaze them, you maximize your chance of the crumb staying on the cake.

This cake can easily be made with almost any of your favorite sugary cereals. If you're using a larger-sized cereal, just be sure to crush or chop the cereal to about the size of a Fruity Pebble.

NO-CHURN KEY LIME GOLDEN GRAHAMS ICE CREAM

YIELD
Serves about 6

When it first came out I will admit I was not a fan of no-churn ice creams. If you are not familiar with them, they use sweetened condensed milk and whipped cream to recreate that creamy ice cream texture. However, the sweetened condensed milk made the ice cream super sweet. And if *I* think it's sweet it has to be *super* sweet. I figured out that you could make a good no-churn ice cream using tart flavors such as lemon or lime, and that works perfectly. The Golden Grahams toffee is a take on cracker toffee but uses the cereal instead. You will have leftover toffee, but I assure you it won't last long.

TOFFEE

4 cups (165 g) Golden Grahams cereal

1 cup (227 g) unsalted butter

1 cup (220 g) packed brown sugar

⅛ tsp salt

KEY LIME ICE CREAM

1 (14-oz [397-g]) can sweetened condensed milk

1 tsp vanilla extract

⅔ cup (160 ml) key lime juice

⅛ tsp salt

2 cups (480 ml) heavy cream, chilled

To make the toffee: Preheat the oven to 350°F (175°C). Line a 10 x 15–inch (25 x 38–cm) pan with heavy-duty aluminum foil. (You don't want to skip that step, because it makes cleaning up a lot easier.) Spray the foil with nonstick baking spray. Spread the cereal as evenly as you can across the pan.

In a medium saucepan over medium-high heat, melt the butter, brown sugar and salt. Once they're combined, bring the mixture to a boil, stirring frequently. Reduce the heat to medium and boil another 5 minutes, stirring frequently. Immediately pour the brown sugar mixture evenly over the cereal in the pan.

Bake for 15 minutes. The brown sugar mixture will be bubbly. Let it cool to room temperature and then move it to the fridge for 20 minutes. Break the toffee into pieces. I usually make this a day ahead.

To make the key lime ice cream: In a large bowl, whisk together the condensed milk, vanilla, key lime juice and salt and set aside.

In the bowl of a stand mixer with the whisk attachment, whip the cream on medium-high speed until firm peaks form, about 2 minutes. Turn off the mixer. Using a rubber spatula, fold about one-third of the whipped cream into the condensed milk and lime mixture until it's combined. Then fold the condensed milk mixture into the whipped cream until it's well blended.

Pour the mixture into a chilled 9 x 5 x 3–inch (23 x 13 x 8–cm) loaf pan and cover it with plastic wrap. Freeze until it's thick and creamy, like soft-serve, about 2 hours. Fold about one-third to half of the Golden Grahams toffee pieces into the mix, doing your best to evenly distribute them. Place the pan back in the freezer and continue to freeze, covered, until the ice cream is solid but scoopable, about 3 hours more.

NOTE: If you do not want to make the toffee, you can just throw in some Golden Grahams or some graham cracker pieces. But I really do think the toffee makes this ice cream extra special, so I encourage you to go for it.

CANDY CRUSH

RECIPES INSPIRED BY MY CANDY ADDICTION

It should come as no surprise that as someone who writes a cookbook called *Holy Sweet!*, I like candy. A lot. If I'm being honest, there is probably not a day that goes by that I don't have candy of some sort. Granted, I'm not sitting down and eating two king-sized candy bars (though I've been there). It's more like a handful of gummy bears or a couple of pieces of red licorice. But it's still daily. Don't you worry, though; I balance it all out with a diet soda. Ha!

This chapter is a collection of my favorite chocolate candies, made into desserts. The Milky Way Pie (page 82) is the lightest, fluffiest dessert you will ever eat. So light, in tact, that after you eat a piece it will feel like you didn't eat anything and you will need another. I say go for it. Whatchamacallit Brownies (page 93) are crispy and chocolaty, with caramel spilling out. Totally worth the sticky fingers. The Snickers Tart (page 86) has pieces of Snickers in it so you know it can't be bad.

I made the Peanut Butter Cup Fudgy Cookies (page 94) over and over again not so much for recipe testing but because my husband's co-workers kept asking for them. They were very sad when all the recipe testing was done for the book. Very sad. I put malted milk balls into cupcake form with the most delicious Swiss meringue buttercream (Malted Milk Ball Chocolate Cupcakes, page 90).

The Almond Joy Flourless Cake (page 89) is somewhat controversial because there are a lot of coconut haters out there. But it is flourless, which means it's gluten-free and therefore a health food. And I added a newer candy bar to the mix, the Cookie Layer Crunch Caramel Magic Bars (page 85), which is a mouthful but oh so yummy.

If your favorite candy bar is represented in this chapter, then yay! If it's not, I encourage you to get creative in the kitchen and see what you can come up with! Feel free to tag me (@bakerpeabody) on social media so I can see.

MILKY WAY PIE

This is the fluffiest and lightest pie you will ever eat, which is a good thing and a bad thing. Good because OMG it's soooo tasty. Bad because you can wolf down three pieces without even feeling full. You do not need to add the salted caramel sauce to the top of the pie, but I recommend it to balance the sweetness.

Preheat the oven to 350°F (175°C).

Mix the cookie crumbs and butter together in a medium bowl. Press the mixture into a 9-inch (23-cm) pie pan. Bake for 10 minutes.

Fill a small saucepan with 2 inches (5 cm) of water and bring it to a simmer. Put the chopped Milky Way bars in a heatproof bowl and set the bowl over the pot of simmering water (the bowl should not touch the water). Heat, stirring occasionally, until the bars are melted.

In a medium saucepan, combine the gelatin and ½ cup (120 ml) of cold water and stir briefly, just to make sure the gelatin and water are combined. Let it stand for 1 to 2 minutes, so the gelatin can bloom. Then turn on the heat to medium and cook, stirring constantly, until the gelatin is completely dissolved, about 5 minutes. This will not smell appetizing, FYI. Remove the pan from the heat. Stir in the vanilla, salt and the remaining ½ cup (120 ml) of water, and whisk until it's all combined.

Put the gelatin mixture in the bowl of a stand mixer fitted with the whisk attachment. Beat in the melted Milky Way bars, cocoa powder and marshmallow creme.

Put the whole bowl in the fridge until the mixture mounds up when dropped from a spoon, about 20 minutes. Fold in the whipped cream and mix until everything is fully incorporated.

Pour the filling into the pie crust. I like to spread mine so the middle of the pie is higher than the edges. Refrigerate for at least 4 hours. Top with salted caramel sauce and extra Milky Way pieces, if using.

> **NOTE**: Feel free to use a store-bought chocolate pie crust for this recipe. I mean, it has gelatin, marshmallows and candy bars in it. Homemade isn't exactly necessary.

1½ cups (129 g) chocolate cookie crumbs

¼ cup (57 g) unsalted butter

2½ (1.84-oz [52.2-g]) Milky Way Original Single bars, finely chopped

1 (2¼-tsp [7-g]) packet powdered unflavored gelatin

1 cup (240 ml) cold water, divided

1 tsp vanilla extract

⅛ tsp salt

1 tbsp (5 g) unsweetened cocoa powder

1 cup (96 g) marshmallow creme

2 cups (480 ml) heavy cream that has been whipped

Salted caramel sauce (optional)

Milky Way mini bars, chopped (optional)

COOKIE LAYER CRUNCH CARAMEL MAGIC BARS

YIELD
Makes about 20

The Cookie Layer Crunch Caramel candy bar is relatively new to the candy bar scene, but it has quickly become a favorite of mine. Shortbread, good. Caramel, good. Chocolate, good. Making them into magic layer bars . . . even better.

Preheat the oven to 350°F (175°C). Spray a 9 x 13–inch (23 x 33–cm) baking pan with nonstick baking spray.

In a medium bowl, combine the finely crushed cookie crumbs and butter. Press the mixture into the bottom of the prepared pan. Pour the condensed milk evenly over the crumb mixture in the pan. Then pour in a layer of caramel sauce. Spread the chocolate chips in an even layer, followed by a layer of caramel bits and a layer of roughly crushed cookie crumbs. Press everything down firmly with a fork.

Bake for 25 minutes or until the top is lightly browned. Cool in the pan, then cut into bars. Store them in an airtight container at room temperature for up to 1 week.

NOTE: There are two kinds of shortbread cookie crumbs here: finely crushed and roughly crushed. The finely crushed cookie crumbs are used for the crust. You can crush the finely crushed crumbs in a food processor or by placing them in a zip-top bag and crushing them with a rolling pin. For the roughly crushed shortbread crumbs you can just break them up with your hands.

1½ cups (150 g) finely crushed shortbread cookie crumbs

½ cup (114 g) unsalted butter, melted

1 (14-oz [397-g]) can sweetened condensed milk

1 cup (240 ml) caramel sauce

1 cup (168 g) milk chocolate chips

1 cup (156 g) caramel bits

1 cup (100 g) roughly crushed shortbread cookie crumbs

SNICKERS TART

YIELD
Serves 6 to 8

Who in their life, at one point or another, has not wanted just a *giant* candy bar? This tart comes pretty close. And yes, there are real Snickers chopped up in it. Because why not? I love the tart dough for this recipe because it is very forgiving, unlike other tart doughs I have worked with in my life. If the candy bar alone won't satisfy, this tart surely will.

To make the tart shell: Preheat the oven to 375°F (190°C).

In a medium bowl, whisk together the flour, sugar and salt. Add the butter and, using a pastry blender, cut it into the flour mixture until it resembles coarse meal. Add the egg yolks and mix lightly until the dough comes together. It might still be a little crumbly, but if you can pinch it with your fingers and it holds together, it's ready.

On a well-floured surface, roll the dough out into a 10-inch (25-cm) circle. Place the circle of dough into an 8-inch (20-cm) tart pan with a removable bottom. Press the dough up along the sides of the pan. Trim away and discard any excess dough.

Put the pan in the refrigerator for about 15 minutes, until the shell is firm. Then bake it for 15 to 20 minutes, until it's cooked and golden. Cool completely before you add the filling.

To make the filling: Place the Snickers pieces upside down inside the cooked tart shell. Set aside.

Put the sugar, water and corn syrup in a small skillet over medium heat and swirl the pan lightly to mix the ingredients. Simmer the mixture until it turns the color of iced tea, about 5 minutes. Remove the pan from the heat and stir in the butter. Add the cream and stir until the filling is smooth. Add the peanuts and mix to incorporate.

Pour the filling evenly into the tart shell over the Snickers pieces. Cool completely, about an hour at room temperature. If you place it in the fridge it will make the caramel cool too fast and will sometimes form crystals, so be patient.

To make the ganache: Put the chocolate chips in a heatproof bowl. In a small saucepan, heat the cream over medium heat until it just starts to boil. As soon as it does, pour it over the chocolate chips. Let everything sit for 5 minutes, then vigorously whisk the chocolate cream mixture until it's smooth. Let it sit for 15 minutes to firm up.

Pour the ganache on top of the tart as evenly as you can. Some will go over the sides; that's fine, it's just chocolate. Cool the tart to room temperature, remove the tart bottom and serve.

NOTE: You can use a food processor to make the tart shell. Process the flour, sugar and salt until they're mixed. Then add the butter and pulse until you have a coarse meal. Add the egg yolks and pulse until the dough comes together.

TART SHELL

1 cup (125 g) all-purpose flour

¼ cup (50 g) granulated sugar

⅛ tsp salt

½ cup (114 g) unsalted butter, cut into small pieces

4 egg yolks

FILLING

1 (1.86-oz [52.7-g]) Snickers bar, cut into 16 pieces

1 cup (200 g) granulated sugar

¼ cup (60 ml) water

¼ cup (60 ml) light corn syrup

¼ cup (57 g) unsalted butter

¼ cup (60 ml) heavy cream

1½ cups (219 g) roasted, shelled, unsalted peanuts

GANACHE

½ cup (84 g) milk chocolate chips

½ cup (120 ml) heavy cream

ALMOND JOY FLOURLESS CAKE

YIELD
Serves about 8

Almond Joy was the one candy bar my parents always tried to steal out of my Halloween bag. Every year when I was little they attempted to convince me that I did not like Almond Joy and that I should give the candy to them instead. This went on for years, until I realized *I do* like Almond Joy. All the flavors of Almond Joy—almonds, chocolate, coconut—are in this flourless cake. If you have never had a flourless cake, you are in for a real treat. And since this cake uses no flour, it is indeed gluten-free, and I'm sure that makes this a health food. So you can eat double the amount, because it's healthy for you.

½ cup (54 g) plus 2 tbsp (14 g) slivered almonds, divided, plus more for garnish (optional)

1 cup (227 g) unsalted butter

1 cup (168 g) finely chopped semisweet chocolate

6 egg yolks

¾ cup (150 g) granulated sugar

8 egg whites, at room temperature

1 cup (93 g) sweetened shredded coconut, finely chopped, plus more for garnish (optional)

Chocolate sauce, for garnish (optional)

Preheat the oven to 325°F (160°C). Position a rack in the center of the oven. Spray the inside of a 9-inch (23-cm) springform pan with nonstick baking spray and line the pan with parchment paper. Don't skip this step or your cake will stick. Sprinkle 2 tablespoons (14 g) of almonds over the bottom of the pan.

Fill a small saucepan with 2 inches (5 cm) of water and bring it to a simmer. Put the butter and chocolate in a small bowl, and set the bowl over the pot of simmering water (the bowl should not touch the water). Heat, stirring often, until the mixture is smooth and all is melted together. Let it cool to room temperature.

In the bowl of a stand mixer with the paddle attachment, beat together on high the egg yolks and sugar until they double in volume and have turned a lighter shade of yellow, about 3 minutes.

Either with a hand mixer or in another clean bowl of the stand mixer with the whisk attachment, beat the egg whites until they're stiff but not dry, about 5 minutes.

Using a rubber spatula, fold the cooled chocolate mixture into the egg yolk mixture. Add one-third of the beaten egg whites and stir very hard to incorporate—this is lightening the batter. This is not the time to be gentle; that comes next.

Now, gently fold the remaining egg whites into the batter. Then gently fold in the coconut and ½ cup (54 g) of almonds.

Pour the mixture into the prepared pan, spreading it evenly. Place the pan on a baking sheet and slide it onto the center rack. Bake for 52 to 54 minutes, or until a wooden skewer inserted in the center comes out fairly clean.

The cake will be puffed up like a soufflé when you take it out . . . but be warned: It *will* fall. It's supposed to fall. You did nothing wrong. It will crack. It always cracks. Again, you have done nothing wrong. Cool the cake in the pan for about 15 minutes, then release the springform and slide the cake onto a plate. Garnish this cake with store-bought chocolate sauce and extra almonds and coconut, if you'd like.

MALTED MILK BALL CHOCOLATE CUPCAKES

YIELD
Makes 20

Years ago on my blog I proposed a new food pyramid—one that included both malted milk balls and Swedish fish, each with their own area on the pyramid. Oddly enough, that did not get approved by the USDA. I'm still working on it, though since tomato sauce on school pizza is now considered a vegetable, I figure I can eventually wear them down. In the meantime I will just go on pretending malted milk balls are their own food group. Which means these cupcakes are part of your daily balanced diet and you can eat as many of them as you like.

To make the cupcakes: Preheat the oven to 350°F (175°C) and line two 12-cup muffin pans with 20 cupcake liners (so some cups will be empty).

In the bowl of a stand mixer with the paddle attachment, mix together the sugar, flour, cocoa powder, malted milk powder, baking powder, baking soda and salt until they're just combined. Add the oil and milk. Mix on low speed until everything is fully incorporated. Add the eggs one at a time, mixing after each addition. Mix in the vanilla. Add the hot water and mix until the batter is evenly combined. This batter is *very* thin.

Fill the cupcake liners just over two-thirds full. Bake for 18 to 22 minutes, until a toothpick inserted in the center of one cupcake comes out clean. Cool the cupcakes completely on a wire rack before frosting.

To make the chocolate Swiss meringue buttercream: Fill a small saucepan with 2 inches (5 cm) of water and bring it to a simmer. Put the egg whites and sugar in the metal bowl of a stand mixer, and set the bowl over the pot of simmering water (the bowl should not touch the water). Heat, stirring occasionally, until the mixture reaches 160°F (71°C).

Transfer the bowl to the stand mixer with the whisk attachment and beat on high speed until you have medium stiff peaks, about 8 minutes. Reduce the mixer speed to medium-low and add the butter 1 tablespoon (14 g) at a time, letting it incorporate into the meringue for a few moments before adding more. Yes, this will take awhile, but it's worth it. Add the vanilla, melted chocolate, malted milk powder and salt, and beat on high for 1 to 2 minutes until the frosting is smooth and creamy.

Frost the cooled cupcakes and top with malted milk balls.

CUPCAKES

2 cups (400 g) granulated sugar

1¾ cups plus 2 tbsp (235 g) all-purpose flour

¾ cup (66 g) unsweetened cocoa powder

¼ cup (30 g) malted milk powder

2 tsp (9 g) baking powder

1½ tsp (7 g) baking soda

1 tsp salt

⅔ cup (160 ml) vegetable oil

1 cup (240 ml) whole milk

2 large eggs, at room temperature

2 tsp (10 ml) vanilla extract

1 cup (240 ml) hot water

CHOCOLATE SWISS MERINGUE BUTTERCREAM

1 cup (240 ml) egg whites (about 9)

2 cups (400 g) granulated sugar

3 cups (681 g) unsalted butter, at room temperature

1 tsp vanilla extract

1¼ cups (210 g) semisweet chocolate chips, melted and cooled slightly

½ cup (65 g) malted milk powder

¼ tsp salt

Malted milk balls, for garnish

WHATCHAMACALLIT BROWNIES

YIELD
Makes about 12

The candy bar with the funny name—but definitely tasty. This bar came out when I was a kid, and I remember feeling so excited that there was a new candy bar (it doesn't take much to excite me, clearly). Originally the bar did not have caramel in it, but it was added a few years later and I definitely think that was the right move. These brownies are sticky and gooey, so make sure to have a napkin ready when you take a bite.

1 box brownie mix of your choice (see the notes below)

1 cup (240 ml) caramel sauce

1½ cups (252 g) milk chocolate chips

1 cup (258 g) peanut butter

1 tbsp (14 g) unsalted butter

1½ cups (44 g) Rice Krispies

Preheat the oven to the temperature indicated on the brownie box. Spray a 9 x 13–inch (23 x 33–cm) baking pan with nonstick baking spray.

Prepare the brownie mix according to the directions on the box. Pour the prepared batter into the pan and even it out with a spatula. Bake for the time recommended on the box, or until a cake tester inserted in the corner of the pan comes out with moist crumbs.

Pour the caramel sauce over the top of the warm brownies and even it out with an offset spatula. Then set them aside to cool.

While the brownies are cooling, place the chocolate chips, peanut butter and butter in a medium saucepan. Cook over low heat, stirring constantly, until everything is melted. Remove the pan from the heat, add the Rice Krispies and mix well. Let this mixture cool for about 3 minutes. Then spread it evenly over the caramel layer, doing the best you can, since it will be sticky.

Refrigerate until the topping is chilled and set, about 2 hours, before cutting into the brownies.

NOTES: You want a brownie mix that makes enough to fit in a 9 x 13–inch (23 x 33–cm) pan. Depending on the brand, this ranges from about 18.3 ounces (519 g) to about 20 ounces (567 g).

Why boxed brownies? I have made this recipe a ton of ways and at the end of the day each person likes their brownies a different way. Some like cakey. Some like fudgy. So I found it easiest to just have people use their favorite brownie mix. That way you get the results you want.

PEANUT BUTTER CUP FUDGY COOKIES

YIELD
Makes 16 to 18

You probably don't have too many cookbooks with a recipe in honor of the author's ex-husband. But I'm not normal. My ex-husband, Justin, started my blog for me in 2005 and taught me how to write HTML (because fifteen years ago that's how you had to write a blog) and ran the back end of my blog—and still does to this day. Part of why I started the blog was as a creative outlet. My ex was known as the picky eater on the blog, because he was. Meat, spaghetti, sloppy Joes and peanut butter and chocolate were about it. So a peanut butter and chocolate cookie seemed right for him. These cookies have a brownie-like texture and are studded with chocolate chips, peanut butter chips and, of course, peanut butter cups.

6 tbsp (84 g) unsalted butter, cut into 6 pieces

1 cup (168 g) coarsely chopped bittersweet chocolate

6 tbsp (66 g) coarsely chopped unsweetened chocolate

3 large eggs

1 cup (200 g) granulated sugar

1 tbsp (15 ml) vanilla extract

⅓ cup (41 g) all-purpose flour

¼ tsp baking powder

¼ tsp salt

28 mini peanut butter cups

¾ cup (126 g) peanut butter chips

¾ cup (126 g) milk chocolate chips

Preheat the oven to 350°F (175°C). Generously spray two baking sheets with nonstick baking spray.

In a microwave-safe medium bowl, add the butter, bittersweet chocolate and unsweetened chocolate. Microwave on high for 1 minute, then stir. Microwave for another 30 seconds and stir again. Continue to microwave in 30-second bursts until everything is melted and the mixture is smooth when you stir it. All in all, it should take about 2 to 2½ minutes.

In the large bowl of a stand mixer fitted with the paddle attachment, beat the eggs and sugar on medium speed for about 3 minutes, until they're fluffy. Add the vanilla and the melted chocolate mixture. Beat on medium speed for about 2 minutes, until the dough is thick and glossy. Remove the bowl from the mixer.

Add the flour, baking powder and salt, and stir just until they're incorporated. Stir in the peanut butter cups, peanut butter chips and chocolate chips. Let the dough rest for 20 minutes at room temperature, which makes it easier to scoop.

Use a 1¾-inch (4.4-cm)-diameter scoop to drop spoonfuls of dough onto the prepared baking sheets, spacing them at least 1½ inches (3.8 cm) apart. Wet your fingertips lightly with water and gently flatten the cookie dough (no need to press hard, just press out the hump). Bake for 10 to 12 minutes, until the tops begin to crack. Cool the cookies for 10 minutes on the baking sheet before removing them to a wire rack.

FAIR ENOUGH

RECIPES INSPIRED
BY STATE FAIR FOODS

Oh, fair food! How I love you. The more outrageous the better, especially if you can get it on a stick. When I lived in Arizona, even though the state fair was not until October, it was usually still so miserably hot that you spent most of your time in the big air-conditioned buildings. I always went because I wanted all the fun fair food, of course.

Then I moved to Washington State and I was surprised by our fairs. They have your classics: caramel apples, funnel cakes, cotton candy, roasted corn, elephant ears and corn dogs on sticks, just like all fairs. But in the Pacific Northwest there is so much fresh and amazing produce that many of the fair food stands feature that as well. So most of the recipes in this chapter include some of the wonderful fruits and vegetables (corn) that our area has to offer. But I tried to make them more over-the-top than what you'll find at our fairs.

You can't have a chapter on fair food and not deep fry something. Nowadays fair vendors are deep frying just about everything you can imagine. They even have a whole show about it. Yes, I watch it. There are two recipes here that have you deep frying some food. Funnel cakes are classic, but I combine them with caramel corn (Caramel Corn Funnel Cakes, page 108) to give you two for one. The other deep fried recipe involves making homemade donuts and then turning them into peach shortcake (Cinnamon Donut Peach Shortcake, page 101). Do *not* miss out on making those. If you fear frying, I'm telling you that recipe alone is worth facing your fears for.

The caramel apples come in the form of Snickerdoodle Caramel Apple Cupcakes (page 111). How about giant cinnamon rolls? Well, I have those, only they sit on top of apple pot pies (Cinnamon Roll Apple Pot Pies, page 98). Lemonade comes in cake form (Raspberry Lemonade Bundt Cake, page 117). Prize-winning jam? That gets turned into Blueberry Limoncello Jam Bars (page 107). Roasted corn comes in the form of bread pudding. Yes, Sweet Corn Bread Pudding (page 113)—and you will love it.

Now you can have a little bit of the fair year round, without all the crowds and outrageous prices.

CINNAMON ROLL APPLE POT PIES

YIELD
Makes 4 mini pot pies

Here's a buttery brown sugar cinnamon crust filled with apple pie filling and topped with a cinnamon roll, all baked up and then slathered in cream cheese frosting. Yes, it's overkill! Yes, it's amazing! This is one of the more complicated recipes in the book, mostly because it has a lot of steps, not because it's hard. But I am here to tell you that it is 100 percent worth making. When I was testing this recipe, I made many, many versions (only slightly different each time) and each time anyone ate one they all had the same response: This recipe alone made the book worth buying. I agree with them.

To make the cinnamon rolls: In a small bowl, add the yeast and warm buttermilk and whisk together. Let the mixture sit for 5 to 10 minutes to bloom. It should look cloudy and the top should have a bubble or two.

In a medium bowl, add the sugar, 2 tablespoons (28 g) of butter, salt, egg and flour. Mix well. Pour the bloomed yeast mixture into the flour mixture. Using your hands, mix the dough until it's well combined. Knead the dough by hand in the bowl for a minute or two. This dough is going to seem more like cookie dough than yeast dough.

Coat a large, clean bowl with oil or nonstick baking spray and add the dough. Cover the bowl with plastic wrap and then a towel. Let the dough rise about 1 hour or until it has doubled in size. If you have a cool house this may take longer than an hour, so do not panic. It may take less time if you have a warm house.

On a lightly floured surface, roll the dough out into approximately a 4 x 9–inch (10 x 23–cm) rectangle. Use a knife or a pizza cutter to cut it in half lengthwise, so you have two strips that are each 2 x 9 inches (5 x 23 cm).

Brush the remaining 3 tablespoons (42 g) of butter all over the dough strips (use it all up). Combine the brown sugar and cinnamon in a small bowl and evenly sprinkle half the mixture over each piece of buttered dough. Carefully, starting from a short side, roll up each of the dough strips. You should now have two giant cinnamon rolls. Cut them each in half so that you have four.

Place them on a baking sheet and cover it with plastic wrap. Leave them at room temperature for at least 30 minutes or until they have doubled in size. While they are rising, prepare the crust and pie filling.

To make the crust: Spray four 5-inch (13-cm) mini pie pans with nonstick baking spray. Really make sure they are good and greased up, since the dough will have sugar in it and it will tend to stick. Set them aside.

(continued)

CINNAMON ROLLS

½ tsp active dry yeast

⅛ cup (30 ml) buttermilk (or whole milk), warm (90–110°F [32–43°C])

2 tbsp (30 g) granulated sugar

5 tbsp (70 g) unsalted butter, melted, divided

⅛ tsp salt

1 large egg

1 cup (125 g) all-purpose flour

¼ cup (55 g) packed brown sugar

1 tbsp (8 g) ground cinnamon

CRUST

2 (9-inch [23-cm]) refrigerated pie crusts

2 tbsp (28 g) unsalted butter, melted

2 tbsp (28 g) packed brown sugar

4 tsp (11 g) ground cinnamon

CINNAMON ROLL APPLE POT PIES
(CONTINUED)

Roll out the pie crusts on a lightly floured surface. Brush the butter all over the pie crusts (use it all up). Combine the brown sugar and cinnamon in a small bowl and evenly sprinkle half the mixture over each buttered crust. Roll the crusts up tightly, as you did with the cinnamon rolls, and slice each one in half. You should have four equal parts of rolled pie crust.

Take one of the sections and cut it into ½-inch (13-mm)-thick slices. Use your hands to push all the slices into a circle, and with a well-floured rolling pin, roll them out in one big circle again, about 6 or 7 inches (15 to 18 cm) in diameter. It should be streaked with cinnamon sugar. Place this crust into one of the prepared pie pans. Using your fingers, press the dough into the pie pan and up the sides.

Repeat the process with the remaining three dough pieces. When you're done, put the crusts in the fridge while you prepare the apple pie filling.

To make the apple pie filling: Put the apples in a medium sauté pan over medium heat. Cook the apples, stirring occasionally, until you start to see juices coming out of them, about 3 to 5 minutes. Then add the sugar and continue to cook until the apples start to get slightly limp, about 5 to 7 minutes. Remove the pan from the heat and place the apples in a medium bowl. Add the apple pie spice and cornstarch, and mix until the apples are coated and the spice and cornstarch are evenly distributed.

To assemble the pot pies: Preheat the oven to 350°F (175°C).

Remove the four pie crusts from the refrigerator. Divide the apple filling evenly among the four pies. Place an uncooked cinnamon roll on top of each pie.

Bake uncovered for 20 minutes. If they start to brown too quickly, you can loosely cover each pie with a piece of aluminum foil to prevent further browning. Remove the pot pies from the oven and let them cool in their pans while you prepare the frosting.

To make the frosting: In the bowl of a stand mixer with the paddle attachment, beat together the cream cheese and butter until they're creamy, about 2 minutes. Mix in the vanilla, salt and milk, then gradually mix in the powdered sugar ½ cup (60 g) at a time. When all the powdered sugar is incorporated, mix for another minute or two until the frosting is nice and fluffy.

Frost the pies while they are still warm and in the pie pans. You can use as much or as little frosting as you want—it's up to you.

APPLE PIE FILLING

3 medium Granny Smith apples, peeled, cored and sliced

⅓ cup (66 g) granulated sugar

1 tsp apple pie spice

½ tsp cornstarch

FROSTING

½ cup (116 g) cream cheese, at room temperature

7 tbsp (98 g) unsalted butter, at room temperature

½ tsp vanilla extract

¼ tsp salt

2–3 tbsp (30–45 ml) whole milk

1½ cups (180 g) powdered sugar

NOTES: Be sure to use active dry yeast for the cinnamon rolls, not rapid rise, because otherwise they just bake up weird. You can use a mixer with the dough hook to knead them, but the amount of dough is so small that I don't think it gets everything mixed properly. I tried it both ways a few times and hand kneading works best.

If you can't find Granny Smith apples, any tart variety will work.

CINNAMON DONUT PEACH SHORTCAKE

YIELD
Makes about 8

The donuts for the shortcakes take some time, but they are soooo worth it. Set aside some weekend time and treat yourself and your family to the way shortcake should be eaten—with a homemade donut. Once you master making these donuts, you will have endless possibilities for all sorts of different donut-shortcake combinations.

To make the donuts: Oil the inside of a large bowl and set aside.

In the bowl of a stand mixer fitted with the dough hook, add the yeast, milk and 2 tablespoons (28 g) of brown sugar. Mix for a minute, then leave the yeast to proof for 10 to 15 minutes, or until the mixture is foamy.

Add the flour, cinnamon, salt, remaining 4 tablespoons (56 g) of brown sugar, eggs and vanilla to the bowl. Mix on low for 2 to 3 minutes, until the dough starts to come together. It may look slightly dry, but that will change when the butter is added. Increase the mixer speed to medium and mix for another 10 minutes, until the dough is soft and smooth. Reduce the mixer speed to low and add the butter 1 tablespoon (14 g) at a time, mixing until each piece is fully incorporated into the dough before adding the next piece, about 3 to 4 minutes total. Once all the butter is in, increase the mixer speed to medium and mix for another 5 to 7 minutes, until the dough is very soft and smooth. Put the dough in the oiled bowl and cover it tightly with plastic wrap. Place it in the fridge to rise overnight or for at least 8 hours.

Line two baking sheets with parchment paper. Turn the dough out onto a well-floured surface. Roll it out to about ½-inch (13-mm) thickness. Using a circle cutter (I used a 3¼-inch [8-cm]-diameter cutter), cut out circles of dough and place them on the baking sheets, leaving room between each one. You should get 12 donuts. You will have more dough leftover, but do not roll it up and make more, as the donuts will not fry well if they are rerolled. Just discard it.

Loosely cover the baking sheets with plastic wrap. Leave the doughnuts to rise for another 20 to 30 minutes. They should get puffy, and when you poke them lightly with your finger it should leave a small indentation that springs back.

Heat 6 cups (1.4 L) of oil in a large heavy-bottomed pot (I use a Dutch oven or deep cast-iron skillet) to 350°F (175°C) (use a thermometer!). Line a baking sheet with paper towels. Place the cinnamon sugar in a small paper bag.

(continued)

DONUTS

1 (2¼-tsp [7-g]) packet active dry yeast

1 cup (240 ml) whole milk, warm (90–100°F [32–38°C])

6 tbsp (84 g) packed brown sugar, divided

3¾ cups (469 g) all-purpose flour

1 tsp ground cinnamon

1 tsp salt

2 large eggs, at room temperature

1 tsp vanilla extract

6 tbsp (84 g) unsalted butter, at room temperature

8 cups (1.9 L) vegetable oil, divided

1 cup (131 g) cinnamon sugar (made from ¼ cup [31 g] ground cinnamon and 1 cup [100 g] granulated sugar)

CINNAMON DONUT PEACH SHORTCAKE (CONTINUED)

Gently lower the donuts, one at a time, into the hot oil. Set a timer for 4 minutes and flip the donut every 30 seconds until it's golden brown. It may take less than 4 minutes. You want to fry one donut at a time, so you can maintain the oil temperature at 350°F (175°C). Check the temperature between each one and adjust by either turning up the heat or adding more oil (to cool it down). Remove the donut from the oil using a slotted spoon and place it on the lined baking sheet. While each donut is still warm, toss it into the paper bag with the cinnamon sugar and shake to coat.

To make the peach filling: Toss the peaches and sugar in a large bowl and let them sit for 30 minutes.

To make the whipped cream: In the bowl of a stand mixer with the whisk attachment, whip the cream and sugar together until stiff peaks form, about 2 minutes.

Cut the donuts in half crosswise. Spoon some peaches and whipped cream on the bottom half of each donut. Place the other half of the donut on top, like an amazing sandwich.

NOTES: There are enough peaches for about eight servings, so you will have four donuts leftover. Eat them.

If you are in a hurry and don't want to make donuts, you can always just slice up store-bought glazed donuts. If you do that, please be sure to find some time to make the homemade donuts at some point because they are the best. THE BEST.

I keep the donuts whole but you can make them with the hole in the middle. Some people like to cut out the hole in the middle to make frying faster.

PEACHES

4 cups (616 g) peeled and sliced fresh peaches

⅓ cup (66 g) granulated sugar

WHIPPED CREAM

2 cups (480 ml) heavy cream

3 tbsp (45 g) granulated sugar

TRIPLE BERRY SCONE COBBLER

YIELD
Serves 6 to 8

Each state fair has a thing it's known for, and Washington State is no exception. I must admit, though, that ours is not what you would expect. It's not deep fried or on a stick. No, it's a scone—and everyone here goes crazy for them. To honor that tradition I made a cobbler with a scone-like texture. The original is served with butter and raspberry jam, but I went for a triple berry cobbler with the three berries you see most here in the summer: blueberries, raspberries and blackberries. This cobbler is going to seem super strange to you. And it is. The first time I tried the recipe fifteen years ago I thought for sure it would be an epic fail. Instead it was a hit. Big hit. It's super messy when you're trying to get it into the pie pan, and it will float up when you add the sugar water . . . but in the end it all comes together. I promise.

1 cup (228 g) unsalted butter, chilled and cut into chunks, divided

1 cup (240 ml) water

1 cup (200 g) granulated sugar

1½ cups (188 g) self-rising flour

⅓ cup (80 ml) milk

Zest of 1 lemon

3 cups (400 g) fresh or frozen mixture of raspberries, blueberries and blackberries

2 tbsp (24 g) sparkling sugar

Vanilla ice cream (optional)

Preheat the oven to 350°F (175°C). Position a rack in the middle of the oven.

Put ½ cup (114 g) of butter in a 10-inch (25-cm) pie pan and put it in the oven to melt, about 4 to 6 minutes.

In a small saucepan, combine the water and sugar and heat over medium heat, stirring occasionally, until the sugar is completely dissolved, about 3 minutes. Set this sugar syrup aside.

In a food processor, pulse together the flour and the remaining ½ cup (114 g) of chilled butter until the mixture resembles fine meal. Add the milk and lemon zest and pulse just until a dough forms. Turn the dough out onto a lightly floured surface and, with a floured rolling pin, roll it into a 9 x 11–inch (23 x 28–cm) rectangle. Scatter the berries evenly over top of the dough. Beginning with a long side, roll up the dough jelly-roll fashion and cut it into 1½-inch (3.8-cm)-thick slices. The slices will come apart and be messy, but don't worry. If fruit falls out (and it will), just throw it on top of the cobbler after it's in the pie pan.

Take the pie pan out of the oven and arrange the dough slices, cut sides up, over the melted butter. Pour the sugar syrup over the slices, soaking the dough. At this point it's going to look like a hot mess and you are going to ask yourself what kind of recipe this is. A weird one . . . but a tasty one.

Bake the cobbler on the middle rack for 45 minutes. Sprinkle the sparkling sugar over the top and bake 15 minutes more, or until the top is golden. Serve warm with ice cream, if you'd like.

BLUEBERRY LIMONCELLO JAM BARS

YIELD
Makes about 24

My friend Heidi makes the best jam. How good? Well, on a whim she entered some of it in our local county fair. Her Blueberry Limoncello Jam won first prize and apparently upset the local jammer community (they are easily upset—don't ever ask them about berry limits at U-pick). New jammers aren't supposed to win, I guess. I was lucky enough to get some of that prize-winning batch. Inspired by the jam, I decided it should be made into jam bars. I'm sure you will find them prize-winning.

Preheat the oven to 350°F (175°C). Spray a 9 x 13–inch (23 x 33–cm) baking pan with nonstick baking spray.

In the bowl of a stand mixer with the paddle attachment, cream the butter and sugar together until they're light and fluffy, about 3 minutes. Add the vanilla and rice flour and beat until everything is incorporated. Add the salt and flour and mix until it comes together with some crumbs, about 3 minutes. Put the dough in the prepared pan and press it evenly over the bottom of the pan.

In a small saucepan, add the blueberry jam and the limoncello and heat over medium heat until it starts to melt, about 2 minutes. Whisk to blend everything. Evenly spread the jam over the dough.

To make the topping: In a small bowl, add the flour, sugar, salt and chilled butter. Rub everything with your fingers until you get a crumbly mixture. Sprinkle this over the jam.

Bake for 50 to 60 minutes (mine took 52 minutes) or until the crumb topping is golden brown. You can top with aluminum foil if it starts to get too brown on top. Remove the pan from the oven and cool on a wire rack (you definitely don't want to eat these hot . . . you will burn your mouth). Cut into squares.

NOTE: If you can't find rice flour, you can substitute almond flour.

JAM BARS

¾ cup (170 g) unsalted butter, at room temperature

⅔ cup (132 g) granulated sugar

2 tsp (10 ml) vanilla bean paste (or extract)

½ cup (79 g) rice flour

¼ tsp salt

2 cups (250 g) all-purpose flour

1 cup (320 g) blueberry jam (home-made or store-bought)

3 tbsp (45 ml) limoncello liqueur

TOPPING

3 tbsp (24 g) all-purpose flour

3 tbsp (45 g) granulated sugar

⅛ tsp salt

2 tbsp (28 g) unsalted butter, chilled and cubed

CARAMEL CORN FUNNEL CAKES

YIELD
Makes about 6

Funnel cakes are actually really simple to make. Which I never realized until one night at 11 p.m., when my husband got up from the couch and proclaimed he was going to make funnel cakes. A statement that made me love him more than I already did. And he understood the correct ratio of powdered sugar to funnel cake, which is a ton. This version combines two fair favorites of funnel cakes and caramel corn.

To make the funnel cakes: In a medium saucepan, add the milk, popcorn and caramel sauce and heat until it just starts to boil, about 3 minutes. Cover the pan and take it off the heat. Let it sit for 20 minutes, then strain out and discard the popcorn. Let the caramel milk cool to room temperature.

In a deep fryer, Dutch oven or heavy skillet, heat 6 cups (1.4 L) of oil to 375°F (190°C). Line a baking sheet with paper towels.

In a large bowl, whisk the eggs and caramel milk until they're fully combined. Add the flour, baking powder and salt and stir until the batter is smooth. It will be thick but still runny. Using either a funnel (use your finger to plug the hole) or a piping bag (hold the bag upright until you're ready to pour the batter), start from the center of the pan with the hot oil and, with a swirling motion, make a 6-inch (15-cm)-diameter funnel cake.

Set a timer for 4 minutes and flip the funnel cake every 30 seconds. Your cakes might be done before the timer goes off, but 4 minutes is what I like to set mine at. You are looking for a golden brown color. Remove the cake to the lined pan. You want to fry one cake at a time, so you can maintain the oil temperature at 375°F (190°C). Check the temperature between each one and adjust by either turning up the heat or adding more oil (to cool it down).

For the toppings, start by making caramel whipped cream. In the bowl of a stand mixer with the whisk attachment, beat the cream on high until stiff peaks form, about 3 minutes. Add ¼ cup (60 ml) of caramel sauce and whip until it's fully incorporated, about 1 or 2 minutes.

Take one funnel cake and place it on a plate. Sprinkle it with powdered sugar (however much you want—go crazy). Top it with some caramel whipped cream, drizzle with plenty of caramel sauce and top it all with pieces of caramel corn.

NOTE: Keep an eye on the oil temperature and try to maintain it at 375°F (190°C). As you fry the cakes, your pan will either get cooler (because you added the batter) or hotter. If the temperature gets too low, you can turn up the heat. It's harder to get the temperature down when the oil heats up. To do this I carefully add more oil and very carefully stir. This will bring the oil temperature down and you can start frying again.

FUNNEL CAKES

1½ cups (360 ml) whole milk

1 cup (8 g) plain popped popcorn

2 tbsp (30 ml) caramel sauce

6 cups (1.4 L) vegetable oil, plus up to 2 cups (480 ml) more

2 large eggs

2 cups (250 g) all-purpose flour

1 tsp baking powder

½ tsp salt

TOPPINGS

1 cup (240 ml) heavy cream

1¼ cups (300 ml) caramel sauce, divided

1 cup (120 g) powdered sugar

1 cup (40 g) caramel corn

SNICKERDOODLE CARAMEL APPLE CUPCAKES

YIELD
Makes 24

Caramel apples are pretty much everywhere at the fair. Sure, it's a gamble whether you will get to keep your teeth or not, but it's worth the risk. These cupcakes have all the best things about caramel apples without the possible tooth loss or having apple juice drip down your arm (maybe that's just me). Though the downside is they don't come on a stick. Then again, if you want to stick these on a stick, feel free. The snickerdoodle part of the cupcakes has nothing to do with the fair. I just really love snickerdoodles. Snickerdoodles also happen to pair really well with caramel apples.

To make the caramel apples: In a heavy skillet over medium heat, melt the butter. Then add the apples and sauté for 1 minute. Add the water and bring it to a boil. Stir in the sugar, reduce the heat to a simmer and cover the pan. Let the apples simmer for 10 to 12 minutes, stirring occasionally, until they are tender. Remove from the heat and stir in the caramel sauce. Mix gently until everything is thoroughly combined.

To make the cupcakes: Preheat the oven to 350°F (175°C). Use ½ cup (114 g) of butter to generously grease two 12-cup muffin pans. Place 1 tablespoon (11 g) of cinnamon sugar in each cup and swirl it around until the sides and bottom are coated.

In a medium bowl, combine the flour and cream of tartar and set aside.

In the bowl of a stand mixer with the paddle attachment, cream together the remaining 1 cup (227 g) of butter and the sugar on medium-high speed for about 3 minutes. Blend in the eggs one at a time, then the egg yolks one at a time, scraping down the sides of the bowl as needed. With the mixer on low speed, add one-third of the flour mixture, then half the buttermilk, then one-third of the flour mixture, the rest of the buttermilk, and the rest of the flour mixture. Mix after each addition just until it's incorporated. Add the vanilla and mix for another 30 seconds. Turn off the mixer and fold in half of the caramel apple pieces. Do your best to distribute them evenly throughout the batter.

Using an ice cream scoop, fill the muffin cups half full with batter. Divide the remaining cinnamon sugar into 12 equal portions (don't get crazy; just do the best you can) and sprinkle some into each cupcake. Swirl the batter with a knife, then top up each cup until it is two-thirds full.

Bake until the cupcakes are just set and pale golden, about 20 to 22 minutes. Let them cool in the pans for about 5 minutes, then remove them to a wire rack to cool completely while you make the frosting.

(continued)

CARAMEL APPLES

2 tbsp (28 g) unsalted butter

2 cups (235 g) apples, peeled, cored and diced small

3 tbsp (45 ml) water

2 tsp (10 g) granulated sugar

½ cup (120 ml) caramel sauce

CUPCAKES

1½ cups (341 g) unsalted butter, at room temperature, divided

1½ cups (243 g) cinnamon sugar (made from ½ cup [62 g] ground cinnamon and 1¼ cups [250 g] granulated sugar), divided

3 cups (375 g) self-rising flour

2 tsp (6 g) cream of tartar

2 cups (400 g) granulated sugar

2 large eggs, at room temperature

4 egg yolks, at room temperature

1 cup (240 ml) buttermilk (or sour cream)

1 tbsp (15 ml) vanilla extract

SNICKERDOODLE CARAMEL APPLE CUPCAKES (CONTINUED)

To make the frosting: Fill a small saucepan with 2 inches (5 cm) of water and bring it to a simmer. Put the egg whites, salt and brown sugar in the metal bowl of a stand mixer, and set the bowl over the pot of simmering water (the bowl should not touch the water). Heat, stirring occasionally, until the mixture reaches 160°F (71°C).

Transfer the bowl to a stand mixer with the whisk attachment and beat on high speed until you have medium stiff peaks, about 8 minutes. Reduce the mixer speed to medium-low and add the butter 1 tablespoon (14 g) at a time, letting it incorporate into the egg whites for a few moments before adding more. At this point you might start to panic because it looks curdled or is not coming together. Don't worry, just keep adding butter. Add the caramel sauce and powdered freeze-dried apples, and beat on high for 1 to 2 minutes until the frosting is smooth and creamy.

Frost the cooled cupcakes and top with the remaining caramel apples.

FROSTING

5 egg whites

¼ tsp salt

1¼ cups (275 g) packed brown sugar

1¾ cups (397 g) unsalted butter, at room temperature

¼ cup (60 ml) caramel sauce

¾ cup (15 g) powdered freeze-dried apples

NOTE: Freeze-dried apples and dried apples are *not* the same thing. Freeze-dried apples are brittle and can be turned into a powder by either placing them in a plastic bag and crushing them with a rolling pin or putting them in a food processor. Most health food stores, and places like Target and Trader Joe's, carry them. You can also find a ton of freeze-dried fruits at Nuts.com.

SWEET CORN BREAD PUDDING

YIELD
Serves about 6

While you usually see people walking around the fair with a giant ear of roasted corn, I thought going the sweet route was more fun. Sweet corn was never something I thought about using in a dessert, until I had it as ice cream and fell in love. The ice cream had a ribbon of black raspberry going through it, and to this day sweet corn and raspberry is a favorite combination of mine. This bread pudding was created with that flavor combo in mind. If you are a fan of sweet corn and have never had it in a dessert, you are in for a treat.

For the bread pudding: Preheat the oven to 350°F (175°C). Spray a 9 x 9–inch (23 x 23–cm) pan with nonstick baking spray.

Cut the corn off the cobs. Put both the kernels and the corn cobs into a large saucepan. Add the cream and bring it to a boil over medium-high heat. As soon as it boils, remove the pan from the heat and cover it. Let the corn steep in the cream for 20 minutes. Strain the mixture and keep the corn kernels in one bowl and the cream in another. Discard the cobs.

In a large bowl, mix together the egg yolks, sugar and honey. Then whisk in the corn-infused cream and the salt. Whisk until the custard is fully mixed.

Tear or cut the croissants into pieces and place half the pieces in the prepared pan. Pour half the custard over the croissants in the pan. Sprinkle half of the reserved corn kernels on top of the custard-soaked croissants. Then spoon on half the raspberry jam. Press down the croissant pieces with your hands until the bread is soaked with the custard. Yes, your hands are going to get messy with custard and jam. Add the remaining croissant pieces, corn and jam.

You now have half the custard mixture left, but the bread pudding may not require all of it. How much custard to pour into the pan will depend on how stale your croissants are. If they are super stale, they will need all the custard. If they are soft, they will most likely need less. You will know you have the right amount of custard when you press down on the croissants and custard pools up at the top.

Cover the bread pudding with aluminum foil. Place that pan in another baking pan that's big enough to hold it without touching the sides. Place both pans in the oven, then add very hot water to the bigger pan until it's halfway up the sides of the smaller pan. Bake for 35 minutes. Remove the foil and bake for another 10 to 20 minutes, until the top is golden. Cool for 10 minutes.

(continued)

BREAD PUDDING

2 ears corn

3 cups (720 ml) heavy cream

6 egg yolks

¾ cup (150 g) granulated sugar

¼ cup (60 ml) honey

⅛ tsp salt

12 large croissants or 16 butterflake rolls, preferably stale

1 cup (325 g) raspberry jam, heated until it has the consistency of syrup

SWEET CORN BREAD PUDDING (CONTINUED)

To make the honey raspberry caramel sauce: In a small saucepan over medium-low heat, mix the honey, brown sugar, cream, butter and salt. Cook, whisking gently, for 5 to 7 minutes, until it thickens. Add the vanilla and raspberry jam and cook another minute to thicken it a bit more. Turn off the heat and cool the sauce slightly. Drizzle it over the bread pudding.

This sauce can be refrigerated in an airtight container for up to 2 weeks. Gently reheat it before serving.

NOTE: You do not have to bake this in a water bath. However, I do recommend it to provide a consistent, steady heat source and ensure even, slow cooking.

HONEY RASPBERRY CARAMEL SAUCE

½ cup (120 ml) honey

1 cup (220 g) packed brown sugar

1 cup (240 ml) heavy cream

¼ cup (57 g) unsalted butter

½ tsp salt

1 tsp vanilla extract

⅓ cup (110 g) raspberry jam

RASPBERRY LEMONADE BUNDT CAKE

YIELD
Serves about 8

Almost every stand at our county fair carries some flavor of lemonade. The local berry around the Pacific Northwest is a marionberry, which is like a tart black raspberry. But they are hard to find for anyone who doesn't live around here. So I decided to make a raspberry lemonade Bundt cake. Since there are so many flavors of lemonade, this is a cake you can change around and make the flavor of your choice. But I am partial to raspberry.

Preheat the oven to 325°F (160°C). Grease and lightly flour a 10-inch (25-cm) fluted tube pan or Bundt pan.

In the bowl of a stand mixer with the paddle attachment, cream together the butter and sugar until they're light and fluffy, about 3 minutes. Add the eggs one at a time, beating well and scraping down the sides and bottom of the bowl after each addition. Add the vanilla and lemon zest and beat for 30 seconds.

In a small bowl, combine the buttermilk and raspberry lemonade and whisk them together. The milk will look clumpy due to the acid in the lemonade. This is normal.

In another small bowl, combine the flour and baking soda. Add one-third of the flour mixture to the butter and sugar mixture and beat for a minute, then add half of the buttermilk and lemonade mixture and beat well. Repeat with another one-third of the flour mixture, the remaining buttermilk and lemonade mixture, followed by the remaining one-third of the flour mixture. Turn off the mixer and fold in the freeze-dried raspberries. Be gentle so the raspberries do not break up into a powder.

Pour the batter into the prepared pan and bake for 70 to 80 minutes, or until a toothpick inserted near the center comes out clean. Cool in the pan for 15 minutes before removing the cake to a wire rack to cool completely while you make the glaze.

To make the glaze: Whisk together the powdered sugar, raspberry lemonade and butter until the mixture is smooth. Add more lemonade if it's too thick. Pour the glaze over the cooled cake, then let it sit for about 30 minutes to set.

NOTE: This cake can be easily converted to any lemonade flavor you like. You can substitute plain lemonade for the raspberry lemonade. And you can change your freeze-dried fruit. All the quantities remain the same.

CAKE

1 cup (227 g) unsalted butter, at room temperature

2½ cups (500 g) granulated sugar

4 large eggs

1 tsp vanilla extract

Zest of 1 lemon

¾ cup (180 ml) buttermilk

¼ cup (60 ml) thawed frozen raspberry lemonade concentrate

3 cups (375 g) all-purpose flour

¼ tsp baking soda

1 cup (140 g) freeze-dried raspberries

GLAZE

2 cups (240 g) powdered sugar, sifted

¼ cup (60 ml) thawed frozen raspberry lemonade concentrate, plus more to thin the glaze

2 tbsp (28 g) unsalted butter, melted

PINEAPPLE UPSIDE-DOWN DUMP CAKE

YIELD
Serves about 12

It doesn't get much easier than a dump cake. Just like the name says, you dump the ingredients into the pan, stir it a little, dump some cake mix and butter on top, bake, and you have cake. It's rather amazing. And addictive. There are tons of ways to make a dump cake, but our local fair has a pineapple upside-down cake in a jar and this dump cake is my ode to that.

Preheat the oven to 350°F (175°C). Spray a 9 x 13–inch (23 x 33–cm) pan with nonstick baking spray.

Dump the cans of pineapple with their juice and 20 maraschino cherries into the pan. Mix it right in the pan with ½ cup (110 g) of brown sugar and spread everything out with a spatula to make it even. Sprinkle the whole box of cake mix over the fruit, doing your best to evenly distribute the mix. Drizzle the butter as evenly as you can over the cake mix.

Place the pineapple rings over the top of the cake mix. Put a maraschino cherry in the middle of each ring. Sprinkle the remaining ¼ cup (55 g) of brown sugar over the top of the pineapple rings.

Bake for 50 to 60 minutes, then remove the cake from the oven and set it on a rack to cool.

NOTES: You can serve dump cake warm or cold. I prefer mine warm for dessert and cold for breakfast. Serve with ice cream or whipped cream for extra yumminess.

2 (20-oz [567-g]) cans crushed pineapple, with their juice

28 maraschino cherries, divided

¾ cup (165 g) packed brown sugar, divided

1 (15.25-oz [432-g]) box yellow cake mix

1 cup (227 g) unsalted butter, melted and cooled slightly

8 pineapple rings, fresh or canned

RECIPES INFUSED WITH BOOZE

I started my status as an amateur mixologist rather young. Thirteen to be exact. Under parental supervision. Hard to believe both my parents were police officers, right? In their defense, I was a super good kid to whom it never even occurred to drink any of the booze I was using to make cocktails. Think Leslie Knope from *Parks and Recreation* as a teenager. That was me.

My father's friend and coworker Elton would sometimes come over on the weekends to get some of my mom's home cooking. Often the adults would have a beer or a cocktail while waiting for dinner. I was sent to the liquor cabinet one day to retrieve some sort of booze. I dragged out a bottle of sloe gin that looked like it had been there since the 1970s—and probably had. I asked what the heck it was and that somehow started a conversation about the different types of cocktails. The next thing you know I had talked my dad and Elton into letting me prepare them cocktails, which became our thing for awhile.

There were some really good cocktails. My dad and Elton really enjoyed the bloody avocado, which was basically a bloody Mary with avocado blended into it. Still a keeper to this day. My orange strawberry banana daiquiri was a hit. So was my version of a mudslide, into which I blended a Hostess Chocolate Donette.

And there were some really bad ones. Really, really bad. Since I wasn't tasting them myself I kind of just had to guess. Sometimes I guessed wrong. Cantaloupe daiquiri was very wrong. There was the grumpy bear, in which I blended blue gummy bears with rum. Interestingly enough, one of our local cider houses makes a hard cider with gummy Life Savers infused in it. Clearly, I was ahead of my time.

I still make cocktails on my blog on Tipsy Tuesdays, especially Jell-O shots. But what I really love is baking with booze. It adds another dimension of flavor that you can only get with alcohol. In this chapter you will find quite the variety of alcohol used. Some recipes, like Kalimotxo Texas Sheet Cake (page 126), have more of a subtle boozy flavor, while Chocolate-Glazed Brown Sugar Amaretto Bundt Cake (page 130) hits you over the head with amaretto in the cake, the syrup and the glaze.

BAILEYS IRISH NUT COFFEE CHEESECAKE

YIELD
Serves about 8

This cheesecake is based on my mom's favorite drink—which doesn't really exist except to her. She went to a restaurant once where they had a signature cocktail that night. It was hot coffee with Baileys Irish Cream liqueur and amaretto, topped with whipped cream and nutmeg. My mom was told it was called Baileys Irish Nut Coffee. Now any place we go she orders this coffee for dessert. And the waiter just stares at her. Every time. Then we have to tell him what it is and how to make it. The best is when they bring her an Irish Nut, which is a shot of Baileys, amaretto, vodka and Kahlúa. What I wouldn't give to watch her down it. She usually just slides it over to me, her lush daughter.

To make the crust: Preheat the oven to 325°F (160°C). Tightly wrap the outside of a 10-inch (25-cm) springform pan with aluminum foil.

Place the cookies in a food processor and grind them to make fine crumbs. Add the brown sugar, cinnamon, butter and salt and pulse until everything is fully combined. Pat the crust mixture into the prepared springform pan. Bake the crust for 5 to 7 minutes.

To make the filling: Preheat the oven to 325°F (160°C).

In the bowl of a stand mixer with the paddle attachment, beat the cream cheese on medium speed until it's very soft and creamy, about 2 to 3 minutes. With the mixer running on low speed, add the brown sugar and beat until it's well combined. Stop the mixer and scrape down the sides and bottom of the bowl. Turn it back on and add the flour. Then add the eggs and egg yolks one at a time, scraping down the bowl at least twice while adding the eggs. Then add the amaretto, Baileys, espresso powder and nutmeg, and again scrape down the bowl.

Pour the batter into the baked crust. Place the springform pan in another baking pan that's big enough to hold it without touching the sides. Place both pans in the oven, then add very hot water to the bigger pan until it's within 1 inch (2.5 cm) of the top of the springform pan. Bake for 1½ to 2 hours. You want your cheesecake to be mostly firm with just the center shaking slightly. Remove the cheesecake from the water bath and place it on a wire rack. Let it set up in the pan for 10 minutes. Take the water bath out of the oven, but leave the oven on.

To make the topping: In a medium bowl, combine the sour cream, brown sugar and espresso powder and mix until they are well incorporated. Spread the topping over the top of the cheesecake. Place it back in the oven and bake for another 5 to 7 minutes. Remove the pan from the oven and let the cheesecake cool to room temperature. Cover with plastic wrap and chill it in the fridge for at least 4 hours before serving.

CRUST

6 oz (170 g) oatmeal cookies (the crunchy kind, not the soft ones)

3 tbsp (42 g) packed brown sugar

1 tsp ground cinnamon

6 tbsp (84 g) unsalted butter

⅛ tsp salt

FILLING

2 lbs (907 g) cream cheese, at room temperature

2 cups (440 g) packed brown sugar

3 tbsp (24 g) all-purpose flour

4 large eggs

2 egg yolks

¼ cup (60 ml) amaretto liqueur

3 tbsp (45 ml) Baileys Irish Cream liqueur (or similar)

1 tbsp (7 g) espresso powder

¼ tsp freshly ground nutmeg

TOPPING

1½ cups (360 ml) sour cream

3 tbsp (42 g) packed brown sugar

1 tsp espresso powder

NOTE: Springform pans are not watertight. The foil wrap will work, but if you bake a lot of cheesecakes, think about getting an inexpensive silicone wrap. The springform pan sits in the silicone holder (it's shaped like a tart pan), and then goes in the water bath.

PIÑA COLADA QUICK BREAD

YIELD
Makes 6 mini loaves

The official cocktail of Puerto Rico, the piña colada, while girlie and frou-frou, is also really delicious. Living in the Seattle area, it gets quite gray in the winter (and spring, fall and summer), so I often daydream about getting away. Since my budget doesn't allow for tropical vacations, tropical cocktails are about all I can get. What's even better is making them into mini loaves and handing them out to friends to add a bit of sunshine to their day as well. Definitely don't forget the little umbrellas.

To make the bread: Preheat the oven to 350°F (175°C). Grease and flour six mini loaf pans.

In the bowl of a stand mixer with the paddle attachment, beat together the eggs, sugar, oil, melted butter, rum and coconut extract on medium speed for 2 minutes.

In another medium bowl, sift and combine the flour, baking soda, baking powder and salt.

With the speed on medium-low, add one-third of the flour mixture to the butter in the stand mixer, then half the buttermilk, one-third of the flour mixture, the other half of the buttermilk and the final third of the flour. Mix the batter until it's just combined. Fold in the pineapple and coconut.

Pour the batter into the prepared mini loaf pans. Bake for 45 to 50 minutes. The loaves will be a dark golden brown when finished. Remove the pans from the oven and place them on a wire rack to cool. While the loaves are still warm, poke several holes in the top of each one with a wooden skewer.

To make the pineapple coconut glaze: In a small saucepan, combine the sugar, pineapple juice, butter, coconut extract and rum. Bring the mixture to a boil over medium-high heat. Boil for about 1 minute, then turn the heat off but leave the saucepan on the burner.

Drizzle the pineapple coconut glaze into the holes you've poked in the loaves. Finish glazing them by using a pastry brush to liberally brush on all the remaining glaze. Sprinkle the tops of the loaves with some coconut and maraschino cherries. Let them sit in the pans for 15 minutes, then carefully remove them. Continue to cool them on a wire rack until they reach room temperature.

NOTE: True piña coladas use light rum, but I prefer spiced rum in this bread. If you are more of a light rum person, feel free to use that instead.

BREAD

4 large eggs

2 cups (400 g) granulated sugar

¾ cup (180 ml) canola oil

¼ cup (57 g) unsalted butter, melted

1 tbsp (15 ml) spiced rum

1 tsp coconut extract

3 cups (375 g) all-purpose flour

½ tsp baking soda

½ tsp baking powder

½ tsp salt

¾ cup (180 ml) buttermilk

½ cup (124 g) canned crushed pineapple, drained

1 cup (93 g) shredded sweetened coconut, plus more for garnish

PINEAPPLE COCONUT GLAZE

1 cup (200 g) granulated sugar

½ cup (120 ml) pineapple juice

1 tbsp (14 g) unsalted butter

1 tsp coconut extract

1 tbsp (15 ml) spiced rum

Maraschino cherries, for garnish

KALIMOTXO TEXAS SHEET CAKE

I know you're looking at the name and wondering what the heck is kalimotxo? When I tell you what it is, you will think it's even stranger. Kalimotxo (no, I don't know how to pronounce that) is a cocktail from Spain that is equal parts red wine and Coke. Served over ice. Weird, I know. But it's soooo good. Think of it as the new rum and Coke. While Texas sheet cake is a staple at many potlucks, I'm guessing not too many of them have cola and red wine in them. Just remember any time you put chocolate and red wine together in a recipe, you are someone's hero.

To make the cake: Preheat the oven to 350°F (175°C). Spray a 10 x 15–inch (25 x 38–cm) baking pan with nonstick baking spray.

In a large saucepan, combine the butter, Coca-Cola, wine and cocoa powder and bring them to a boil over medium heat. Remove the pan from the heat and set it aside.

In a medium bowl, combine the flour, sugar, baking soda and salt. Add the dry ingredients to the cocoa mixture and mix until everything is fully combined. Stir in the buttermilk and mix until the batter is smooth.

Pour the batter into the prepared pan and spread it as evenly as possible. Bake for 20 to 25 minutes, or until a toothpick inserted in the center comes out clean. Cool the cake in the pan on a wire rack while you make the icing.

To make the icing: In a small saucepan, melt the butter over medium heat. Add the Coca-Cola and cocoa powder. Bring the mixture to a boil. Remove the pan from the heat.

Whisk in the powdered sugar and salt until the mixture is smooth. Add the wine and whisk again until it's smooth. Pour the icing over the warm cake. Cool the cake completely on a wire rack before slicing.

NOTE: I recommend using either a Syrah or a Cabernet Sauvignon for the red wine. You want a more bold red wine since you are only using a few tablespoons in both the cake and the icing.

CAKE

1 cup (227 g) unsalted butter, cubed

1 cup (240 ml) Coca-Cola (or any regular cola, *not* diet)

3 tbsp (45 ml) red wine

¼ cup (22 g) unsweetened cocoa powder

2 cups (250 g) all-purpose flour

2 cups (400 g) granulated sugar

1 tsp baking soda

½ tsp salt

½ cup (120 ml) buttermilk (or sour cream)

ICING

½ cup (114 g) unsalted butter, cubed

¼ cup (60 ml) Coca-Cola (or any regular cola, *not* diet)

3 tbsp (16 g) unsweetened cocoa powder

3¾ cups (450 g) powdered sugar

⅛ tsp salt

3 tbsp (45 ml) red wine

BOURBON PEACH UPSIDE-DOWN CAKE

Bourbon and peaches go together like . . . well, bourbon and peaches. So putting them together in a cake makes total sense. At least to me. This is a pretty simple cake, and therefore it's important to use good fresh peaches. You can use frozen but it just won't be the same. The same goes for your bourbon. Pick a good one. Don't know a good one? Ask your friendly liquor store employee or family lush.

Preheat the oven to 350°F (175°C).

Melt ¼ cup (56 g) of butter and pour it into an ungreased 9-inch (23-cm) round cake pan. Sprinkle it with the brown sugar. Arrange the peach slices in a single layer over the sugar. Drizzle 4 tablespoons (60 ml) of bourbon over the peaches.

In the bowl of a stand mixer with the paddle attachment, cream together the sugar and the remaining ½ cup (114 g) of butter until they're light and fluffy, about 3 minutes. Beat in the egg and the remaining 3 tablespoons (45 ml) of bourbon.

In a small bowl, combine the flour, baking powder and salt. Add it to the creamed mixture in thirds, alternating with the milk and beating well after each addition. Spoon the batter over the peaches in the pan.

Bake for 45 to 50 minutes, or until a toothpick inserted in the center comes out clean. Cool for 10 minutes before inverting the cake onto a serving plate. Serve the cake warm with ice cream, if you'd like.

¾ cup (170 g) unsalted butter, at room temperature, divided

½ cup (110 g) packed brown sugar

2 cups (308 g) peeled, sliced fresh peaches

7 tbsp (105 ml) bourbon, divided

¾ cup (150 g) granulated sugar

1 large egg

1¼ cups (156 g) all-purpose flour

1¼ tsp (6 g) baking powder

¼ tsp salt

½ cup (120 ml) whole milk

Ice cream (optional)

CHOCOLATE-GLAZED BROWN SUGAR AMARETTO BUNDT CAKE

YIELD
Serves 10 to 12

Some like a butter-based pound cake, others are cream cheese pound cake people. I like a combo of both. This cake is a mash-up of a reader's grandmother's recipe, one of my favorite bloggers (Sprinkle Bakes) Heather's recipe and my recipe. This cake is overkill: It is bathed in a boozy syrup and then covered in a thick chocolate amaretto glaze. Do you need both? I say yes. And speaking of overkill, there is amaretto in the cake, the syrup and the glaze.

To make the Bundt cake: Preheat the oven to 325°F (160°C). Spray a 12-cup (2.8-L) Bundt pan with nonstick baking spray.

In the bowl of a stand mixer with the paddle attachment, cream together the butter, cream cheese and brown sugar until they're light and fluffy, about 5 minutes. Add the eggs one at a time, scraping down the sides and bottom of the bowl after each addition. Beat in the vanilla and almond extracts and the amaretto until all the ingredients are thoroughly combined.

In a medium bowl, whisk together the flour, baking powder and baking soda. With the mixer on low speed, beat one-third of the flour mixture into the batter, then half the buttermilk, then one-third of the flour mixture, then the rest of the buttermilk, then the rest of the flour mixture.

Pour the batter into the prepared pan. Bake for 1 hour or until a toothpick inserted in the center of the cake comes out clean. Cool the cake in the pan for 5 minutes. Then turn it out onto a cooling rack to cool completely. Place the cooling rack on a large baking sheet to catch the syrup and glaze.

To make the syrup: Combine the sugar, butter and water in a small saucepan and place it over medium heat. Stir until the sugar melts, about 5 minutes. Remove the pan from the heat and whisk in the amaretto and salt. Using a pastry brush, liberally brush the syrup over the surface of the cooled cake and let it firm up for about 15 minutes before adding the glaze.

To make the glaze: Melt the butter over low heat in a medium saucepan. Add the amaretto, cocoa and powdered sugar and whisk until the mixture is glossy. Remove the pan from the heat and whisk in the almond extract and salt. Let it cool slightly, then pour the glaze over the cake, letting it pool in the center. Let the cake sit for at least 30 minutes before slicing.

BUNDT CAKE

½ cup (114 g) unsalted butter, at room temperature

½ cup (116 g) cream cheese, at room temperature

2¼ cups (495 g) packed brown sugar

5 large eggs, at room temperature

1 tsp vanilla extract

1 tsp almond extract

¼ cup (60 ml) amaretto liqueur

3 cups (375 g) all-purpose flour

½ tsp baking powder

½ tsp baking soda

1 cup (240 ml) buttermilk

AMARETTO BUTTER SYRUP

⅓ cup (66 g) granulated sugar

¼ cup (57 g) unsalted butter

¼ cup (60 ml) water

¼ cup (60 ml) amaretto liqueur

⅛ tsp salt

CHOCOLATE AMARETTO GLAZE

½ cup (114 g) unsalted butter

⅓ cup (80 ml) amaretto liqueur

½ cup (44 g) high-quality unsweetened dark cocoa powder

2 cups (240 g) sifted powdered sugar (sifted then measured)

2 tsp (10 ml) almond extract

¼ tsp salt

DARK AND STORMY GINGER COOKIES

YIELD
Makes 22 to 24

My friend Lindsey and her husband love a good Tiki bar. So much so that they have one in their house—and spend their vacations seeking them out. These Dark and Stormy Ginger Cookies were made for her, since the first time I ever had the drink was in a Tiki bar in California. The cocktail is made with dark rum and ginger beer and served with a lime wedge. The cookies have both the ginger and rum in them and are rolled in a lime sugar mixture and then topped with more rum in the glaze. You just need to put on a grass skirt and you are good to go.

To make the lime sugar: In a medium bowl, mix the lime zest and sugar. Rub the zest into the sugar with your hands. You can then sift out the zest or leave it in. Set aside.

To make the cookies: Mix the flour, ginger, baking soda and salt in a large bowl. Set aside.

In the bowl of a stand mixer with the paddle attachment, beat together the butter and brown sugar until they're light and fluffy, about 3 minutes. Add the molasses, egg, vanilla and rum, and beat well. Gradually beat in the flour mixture on low speed until the dough is well mixed. Use your hands to press the dough into a thick, flat disk. Wrap it in plastic wrap and refrigerate for 4 hours or overnight.

Preheat the oven to 350°F (175°C). Pour the lime sugar into a shallow pan.

Shape the chilled dough into 1-inch (2.5-cm) balls and roll them in the lime sugar. Place the balls 2 inches (5 cm) apart on an ungreased baking sheet. Bake for 8 to 10 minutes, or until the edges of the cookies just begin to brown. Remove the cookies to wire racks and cool them completely.

To make the glaze: In a small bowl, whisk together the rum and powdered sugar. If the glaze is too thick add more rum. If it's too thin add more powdered sugar. Drizzle the glaze over the cookies. You can store the cookies in an airtight container for up to 5 days.

LIME SUGAR

Zest of 1 lime

¼ cup (50 g) granulated sugar

COOKIES

2½ cups plus 1 tbsp (320 g) all-purpose flour

1 tbsp (5 g) ground ginger

1 tsp baking soda

¼ tsp salt

¾ cup (170 g) unsalted butter, at room temperature

¾ cup (165 g) firmly packed brown sugar

½ cup (120 ml) molasses

1 large egg

½ tsp vanilla extract

3 tbsp (45 ml) dark rum

GLAZE

1–2 tbsp (15–30 ml) dark rum

½ cup (60 g) powdered sugar

JACK AND COKE BLONDIES

YIELD
Makes 12 to 16

Back before my husband and I started taking in special needs spaniels, we used to pick a different NHL city each year and visit the hockey arena. In 2014 we decided to go to Nashville and fell in love with the area. No visit to Nashville is complete without heading out to the Jack Daniel's distillery. Jack and Coke always reminds me of that trip. (Side note: Everywhere we went in Nashville people were praying before mealtime and then having a cocktail with the meal—especially brunch. To which I was told by a Nashville native, "We love us some Jesus, but Jesus loves us drinking." Alrighty then.) These blondies are made with whiskey, swirled with a Coca-Cola cream cheese filling, all covered in a Jack and Coke glaze.

To make the cheesecake swirl: In a medium saucepan, bring the Coca-Cola to a boil over high heat. Reduce the heat to medium and let it simmer until the soda has reduced to about ⅓ cup (80 ml) of syrup. Remove the pan from heat and let the syrup cool.

In the bowl of a stand mixer fitted with the paddle attachment, beat together the cream cheese, sugar, flour, egg and vanilla until they're smooth and creamy, about 2 to 3 minutes. Add in the cola syrup and beat until they are fully combined. Set aside.

To make the blondies: Preheat the oven to 325°F (160°C). Line a 9 x 9–inch (23 x 23–cm) baking pan with parchment paper and spray it with nonstick baking spray.

In the bowl of a stand mixer with the paddle attachment, cream together the butter, sugar and brown sugar until they're light and fluffy, about 3 minutes. Add in the eggs, vanilla and whiskey, and mix well until everything is fully combined. Add the flour, baking powder and salt, and mix until they're just combined.

Place half the blondie batter in the prepared pan and smooth it out to cover the bottom of the pan. Place spoonfuls of the cheesecake batter on top of the blondie batter, but do not spread it out. Place spoonfuls of the remaining blondie batter around the cheesecake batter. If necessary, smooth out the top of the batters so they are mostly even.

Bake for 40 to 50 minutes, or until a toothpick inserted in the middle comes out mostly clean, or with just a few moist crumbs. Set the pan on a wire rack to cool to room temperature. When it's cool, cut the blondies into 12 to 16 bars, depending on how big you want them.

To make the glaze: In a small bowl whisk together the whiskey, Coca-Cola and sugar until they are smooth. Drizzle the glaze over the bars. Store the blondies in an airtight container in the fridge for up to 3 days.

CHEESECAKE SWIRL

1 cup (240 ml) Coca-Cola (or any regular cola, *not* diet)

1 lb (450 g) cream cheese, at room temperature

2 tbsp (30 g) granulated sugar

1 tbsp (8 g) all-purpose flour

1 large egg

½ tsp vanilla extract

BLONDIES

¾ cup (170 g) unsalted butter, at room temperature

½ cup (100 g) granulated sugar

¾ cup (165 g) packed brown sugar

2 large eggs

½ tsp vanilla extract

¼ cup (60 ml) Jack Daniel's Tennessee Whiskey (or similar)

1¾ cups (219 g) all-purpose flour

1¼ tsp (6 g) baking powder

½ tsp salt

GLAZE

2 tbsp (30 ml) Jack Daniel's Tennessee Whiskey (or similar)

2 tbsp (30 ml) Coca-Cola (or any regular cola, *not* diet)

1 cup (120 g) powdered sugar

BANANAS FOSTER ICE CREAM PIE

YIELD
Serves 6 to 8

If you have ever seen Bananas Foster prepared tableside, it's something to see. All the flames! I don't make you set anything on fire in this recipe because I'm accident-prone and enjoy not setting myself or others on fire. You're welcome. Even with no flambé, though, you get all the flavors of Bananas Foster, and I finally got to use the banana liqueur that has been in my cabinet for years. Win-win.

To make the crust: Generously spray a 9-inch (23-cm) pie dish with nonstick baking spray.

In the bowl of a food processor, pulse the graham crackers and sugar cones until they are finely crushed. Transfer the crumbs to a medium bowl and add the sugar and melted butter. Mix until they're fully combined. The mixture will look like wet sand.

Press the crumb mixture into the bottom and up the sides of the prepared pie dish. Use the bottom of a glass or a measuring cup on the bottom of the crust and your fingers up the sides to really make it all compact. Put the crust in the refrigerator for 30 minutes. This is a no-bake crust.

To make the filling: In a medium skillet over medium heat, melt the butter and sugar, stirring to combine them. Add the bananas and sauté them until they are lightly browned, flipping the slices once. Sprinkle them with cinnamon. Add the banana liqueur and rum to the pan, raise the heat to medium-high and cook the mixture down for about 3 to 4 minutes. Set the Bananas Foster mixture aside.

In a large bowl, mix together the vanilla ice cream and two-thirds of the Bananas Foster mixture until they are fully combined. Do your best to distribute the bananas throughout the ice cream. Pour the mixture into the chilled pie crust. Cover it with plastic wrap and place in the freezer for at least 4 hours. Put the remaining Bananas Foster mixture in an airtight container and put it in the fridge.

When the pie is frozen, remove it from the freezer. Take out the leftover Bananas Foster mixture from the fridge and put it in a small sauté pan. Reheat the mixture over medium heat until it is just warm. Set aside.

To make the topping: In the bowl of a stand mixer with the whisk attachment, whip the cream and brown sugar together until stiff peaks form, about 3 minutes. Top the entire pie with whipped cream, then drizzle the warmed Bananas Foster mixture on top of that.

NOTE: If you don't have a food processor, put the graham crackers and sugar cones in a zip-top bag and crush them with a rolling pin.

CRUST

12 graham crackers

3 sugar ice cream cones

¼ cup (50 g) granulated sugar

6 tbsp (84 g) unsalted butter, melted

BANANAS FOSTER FILLING

3 tbsp (42 g) unsalted butter

¼ cup (55 g) packed dark brown sugar

3 bananas, peeled and sliced

½ tsp ground cinnamon

1 tbsp (15 ml) banana liqueur

¼ cup (60 ml) dark rum

4 cups (530 g) vanilla ice cream, softened

TOPPING

1 cup (240 ml) heavy cream

3 tbsp (42 g) packed brown sugar

BROWN BUTTER PEACH MELBA CRUMB CAKE

YIELD
Serves 14 to 16

For years as a kid I believed peach melba was a cocktail and not a dessert, because that's what my neighbor told me. When I found out it was just peaches with raspberry sauce and ice cream, I thought it sounded way better as a cocktail. Which is why during my cocktail-making phase as a teenager I created the peach melba—peach schnapps, Chambord and vodka. I didn't want my neighbor to be a liar. This cake is definitely better than the ordinary dessert version of peach melba, and incorporates my cocktail (minus the vodka) as well. You will get more jam than you need for the cake, but throw it on some ice cream and it's all good. The brown butter adds an extra layer of flavor and depth that takes this crumb cake to another level.

To make the brown butter streusel: Preheat the oven to 350°F (175°C). Line a baking sheet with parchment paper.

Put the butter in a small saucepan and place it over medium heat, stirring occasionally, until the butter has melted. Continue to cook until the butter begins to foam, smells nutty and turns a deep golden brown, about 2 to 3 minutes. Remove from the heat and pour the butter in a large bowl. Add the sugar, salt, vanilla and flour and mix well to combine. Using your hands, break up any large lumps.

Spread the mixture evenly over the baking sheet and bake until the streusel is lightly golden and toasty, 10 to 15 minutes. Remove and cool completely. You can make the streusel a day ahead or two and store it in an airtight container.

To make the peach melba jam: Put the peaches, raspberries, Chambord, schnapps, sugar, vanilla and salt in a large skillet over medium heat. Bring to a boil, stirring occasionally, then roughly mash everything with a wooden spoon. Continue to cook, stirring frequently, for 15 minutes, or until the jam is thick. Transfer to an airtight container and chill in the refrigerator. You can also make the jam a day or two ahead.

(continued)

BROWN BUTTER STREUSEL

11 tbsp (154 g) unsalted butter, cut into 1-tbsp (14-g) pieces

1 cup (220 g) packed brown sugar

1 tsp salt

1 tsp vanilla bean paste (or extract)

1½ cups plus 1 tbsp (196 g) all-purpose flour

PEACH MELBA JAM

3 cups (462 g) diced fresh (or frozen) peaches

1 cup (123 g) fresh (or frozen) raspberries

2 tbsp (30 ml) Chambord Black Raspberry liqueur

2 tbsp (30 ml) peach schnapps

1 cup (200 g) granulated sugar

½ tsp vanilla bean paste

½ tsp salt

BROWN BUTTER PEACH MELBA CRUMB CAKE (CONTINUED)

To make the cake: Preheat the oven to 350°F (175°C). Position a rack in the center of the oven. Spray a 9 x 13–inch (23 x 33–cm) baking pan with nonstick baking spray.

In a medium bowl, sift together the flour, baking powder, baking soda and salt. Set aside.

In the bowl of a stand mixer fitted with the paddle attachment, cream the butter until it's smooth, about 2 or 3 minutes. Scrape down the sides of the bowl, then add the sugar. Beat until the mixture is light and fluffy, about 3 minutes. Add the eggs one at a time, beating well after each addition and scraping the bowl as needed. Add the sour cream, buttermilk and vanilla and beat until they're just incorporated. Add the dry ingredients in three portions, scraping down the bowl before each addition and beating only until each addition is just incorporated. Do not over-mix!

Pour half of the cake batter into the prepared pan. Spread the batter evenly in the pan. Spread ½ cup (165 g) of the peach melba jam on top of the batter. Spoon the remaining batter over the peach melba jam. Spread the remaining ½ cup (165 g) of peach melba jam on top of the batter. Swirl the batter with a knife. Smooth the top of the cake with a rubber spatula to make it flat. Sprinkle the streusel topping evenly over the top of the cake.

Bake for 1 hour, or until a toothpick inserted in the center of the cake comes out clean. Cool the cake in the pan on a wire rack for 30 minutes.

To make the icing: In a small bowl, mix the peach melba jam, Chambord, schnapps and powdered sugar together until they're smooth. If you want thicker icing, add more sugar. If you want thinner icing, add more peach melba jam.

Pour the icing over the top of the cake and let it set in the pan for about 30 minutes. Serve with ice cream, if you'd like.

CAKE

3½ cups (438 g) all-purpose flour

1 tsp baking powder

1½ tsp (7 g) baking soda

½ tsp salt

1 cup (227 g) unsalted butter, at room temperature

2½ cups (500 g) granulated sugar

4 large eggs

1 cup (240 ml) sour cream

1 cup (240 ml) buttermilk

1½ tsp (7 ml) vanilla bean paste

1 cup (330 g) peach melba jam

1½ cups (150 g) brown butter streusel

ICING

6 tbsp (124 g) peach melba jam

1 tbsp (15 ml) Chambord Black Raspberry liqueur

1 tbsp (15 ml) peach schnapps

1½ cups (180 g) powdered sugar

Vanilla ice cream (optional)

HOLLY
JOLLY

RECIPES TO CELEBRATE THE HOLIDAYS

I've always loved the holidays, but it was not until my husband and I adopted a Cavalier King Charles Spaniel named Holly Belle that they really started feeling extra special.

The day after American Thanksgiving in 2015 we put up our tree. It was nighttime and all the lights were on in the house. None of the dogs seemed remotely interested in what we were doing. We headed to bed. The next morning when the house was still pitch dark, I turned on the tree lights first. Holly leaped onto the couch like she was Max from the Grinch getting onto the sleigh, and ran to the edge of the couch where the tree was.

And there she sat in total wonder and awe. She was staring at the lit tree like newborns look at all new things, but with an extra special glimmer in her eye. I realized that not being an indoor dog, she had never seen a Christmas tree before.

She did this every day for a week. I would come down, turn on the tree, and she would run over and just stare at it for hours. I told my husband about it and got the "sure, okay" kind of comments. I get it, she's a dog. But that weekend he was up first and turned the tree on in the dark morning, and sure enough she ran to the edge of the couch and stared at the tree, just as she had been doing for me. We kept the tree up (it's fake) until April that year because we didn't want to disappoint her by taking it down.

Holly, like most of the spaniels we take in, had congestive heart failure, so we knew her time was limited. We put the Christmas tree up at the end of September that year. Just like the year before she ran to the edge of the couch and stared at the lights with pure joy in her eyes. She became ill in early October, but she left this world surrounded by love and staring at that tree with wonder.

You may be thinking, why on Earth are you telling such a sad story for the intro to a holiday chapter? Because it's not sad to me. Holly Belle taught me and my husband a lot that year. It's because of her that we dedicate our lives to taking in Cavaliers and English Toy Spaniels with heart disease. Holly taught us that time is precious. To make the most of it and celebrate the little and big things in life. To be in total awe of simple things like Christmas tree lights.

Around here we now go all out at holiday time. We celebrate Canadian Thanksgiving, so it's okay that our tree goes up in October. Our UPS man thinks we are a little crazy, but our friends know why we do it.

This chapter is filled with recipes that cover all the holiday flavors, including a visually stunning Peppermint Bark Red Velvet Layer Cake (page 144), easy-to-make Fruitcake Monkey Bread (page 150) and luscious Eggnog Crème Caramel (page 160), just to name a few. I hope you make all the recipes in this chapter and that they bring you as much joy as the lights on a Christmas tree brought Holly Belle.

PEPPERMINT BARK RED VELVET LAYER CAKE

YIELD
Serves 10 to 12

Visually, a red velvet cake is something to behold—usually a very deep red color against stark white frosting. Most people are used to cream cheese frosting with their red velvet cake, but I found through trial and error that cream cheese and peppermint just don't go that well together. I mean, don't get me wrong, cream cheese frosting does go with just about everything. But in this case I found that with peppermint, the Swiss meringue buttercream works much better.

To make the cake: Preheat the oven to 350°F (175°C). Line three 8-inch (20-cm) round cake pans with parchment paper circles and spray them with nonstick baking spray.

In a medium bowl, sift the flour, baking soda and cocoa together.

In the bowl of a stand mixer with the paddle attachment, cream the eggs, sugar, oil and vinegar. Add the flour mixture to the creamed ingredients while the mixer is running. Then slowly add the buttermilk, then the vanilla and the food coloring. Beat just until everything is well mixed.

Pour the batter into the prepared pans and bake for about 25 minutes. Press lightly; if the cake is spongy, it's done. Let the cakes cool for 5 minutes, them remove them from the cake pans and cool on a wire rack until they're completely cool and ready to frost.

To make the Swiss meringue buttercream: Fill a small saucepan with 2 inches (5 cm) of water and bring it to a simmer. Put the egg whites and sugar in the metal bowl of a stand mixer and set the bowl over the pot of simmering water (the bowl should not touch the water). Heat, stirring occasionally, until the mixture is 160°F (71°C) or hot to the touch.

Transfer the bowl to a stand mixer and beat on high speed with the whisk attachment until you have medium stiff peaks, about 8 minutes. Reduce the mixer speed to medium-low and add the butter a piece at a time, letting it incorporate into the meringue for a few moments before adding more. Add the peppermint extract, melted white chocolate and salt, and beat on high for 1 to 2 minutes, until the frosting is smooth and creamy.

To assemble the cake: Set one cake layer on a turntable cake stand. Top with ¾ cup (180 ml) of frosting and spread out the frosting to the edge of the cake. Top with one-third of the peppermint bark pieces. Top with a second cake layer. Top with ¾ cup (180 ml) of frosting and spread out the frosting to the edge of the cake. Top with one-third of the peppermint bark pieces. Place the last cake layer on top.

Use an offset spatula to frost the cake all over with the buttercream, first making a thin coat to seal in the crumbs. Once your crumb coat is applied, place the cake in the fridge for 30 minutes to firm up. Then cover the cake completely with another layer of frosting, which now will be crumb free. Add the remaining peppermint bark pieces to the top of the cake.

CAKE

2½ cups (300 g) cake flour

1 tsp baking soda

2 tbsp (11 g) unsweetened cocoa powder

2 large eggs

1½ cups (300 g) granulated sugar

1½ cups (360 ml) vegetable oil

1 tsp white vinegar

1 cup (240 ml) buttermilk

1 tsp vanilla extract

¼ cup (60 ml) red food coloring

SWISS MERINGUE BUTTERCREAM

1 cup (240 ml) egg whites (about 9)

2 cups (400 g) granulated sugar

3 cups (681 g) unsalted butter, cubed, at room temperature

1 tbsp (15 ml) peppermint extract

½ cup (84 g) finely chopped white chocolate, melted and slightly cooled

¼ tsp salt

1 cup (173 g) roughly chopped white chocolate peppermint bark

NOTES: This cake uses a good amount of red food coloring. You do not have to use that much, but know that you will not have as red a cake.

If you are unfamiliar with a crumb coat, it's a thin coating of frosting that is spread over all the cake to pick up all the little crumbs. And I can assure you that it is very necessary.

MAPLE BAR PUMPKIN CHEESECAKE BREAD PUDDING

YIELD
Serves about 16

This recipe has so much goodness going on, it might make your head spin. Maple bar donuts. Yum. Pumpkin cheesecake custard. Yum. Bread pudding made from maple bar donuts and pumpkin cheesecake custard. Double yum. Then it's all topped with a maple glaze. While it might seem too sweet because you are using donuts as a base, the cream cheese in the custard really helps to cut that. Also, is anything too sweet? Probably not to the author of a book called *Holy Sweet!*.

To make the bread pudding: Preheat the oven to 350°F (175°C). Position a rack in the middle of your oven. Spray a 9 x 13–inch (23 x 33–cm) baking dish with nonstick baking spray.

In a medium bowl, combine the cream cheese and sugar and mix until the cream cheese is smooth.

In the bowl of a stand mixer with the paddle attachment, combine the eggs, pumpkin purée, milk, cream, vanilla, salt and pumpkin pie spice. Beat until the mixture is smooth. Add the cream cheese mixture and beat until you have a smooth custard.

Pour ½ cup (120 ml) of the custard in the bottom of the baking dish. Tilt and swirl the dish until the bottom is completely covered with a thin layer of custard. Layer half the maple bar donut cubes on top of the custard. Pour half of the remaining custard over the maple bars. Add the remaining maple bars and the rest of the custard. Press down with your hands to make sure the maple bars get soaked with the custard. Let the pan stand for 15 minutes.

Place your baking dish in another baking pan that's big enough to hold it without touching the sides. Put both pans in the oven, then add very hot water to the bigger pan until it's halfway up the sides of the smaller pan. Bake for 1 hour to 1 hour and 15 minutes, or until the top is nicely browned and the custard has risen to the top of the baking dish. Check the water bath occasionally and add more water if needed. Do not let the water evaporate from the water bath.

Carefully remove the baking dish and the water bath from the oven. Put the pan with the bread pudding on a rack to cool for at least 1 hour.

To make the maple glaze: In a medium bowl, whisk together the powdered sugar, maple syrup and cream. Keep whisking until the mixture is smooth. Pour the glaze over the bread pudding. Let it set at least 10 minutes before serving.

BREAD PUDDING

1 lb (450 g) cream cheese, at room temperature

1 cup (200 g) granulated sugar

6 large eggs

1 (15-oz [425-g]) can pumpkin purée

1 cup (240 ml) whole milk

2 cups (480 ml) heavy cream

1 tsp vanilla extract

¼ tsp salt

1 tbsp (8 g) pumpkin pie spice

10 maple bar donuts, cut into cubes, slightly stale if possible

MAPLE GLAZE

1 cup (120 g) powdered sugar

¼ cup (60 ml) maple syrup

¼ cup (60 ml) heavy cream

NOTES: Buy a dozen maple bars. The recipe only calls for ten, but if you live in a home like mine, your husband will come and eat some of them.

Make sure you buy plain pumpkin purée, not pumpkin pie mix, which has added sugar and spices.

Pumpkin pie spice is a mixture of ground cinnamon, ginger, nutmeg, allspice and cloves. A little more of the first two and a little less of the others. You can always make your own.

WHITE CHOCOLATE CANDY CANE CHEESECAKE TARTS

YIELD
Makes 8

I worked in a bakery for a bit and was in charge of making cheesecakes. I thought it would kill my desire to want to eat cheesecakes (my brother could never eat fried chicken after working at a fast food place), but instead it just made me get more creative in my cheesecake making. At holiday time I created a candy cane cheesecake that people swooned for. This is a scaled-down version of that cheesecake in portable tart form.

To make the cocoa crust: Preheat the oven to 250°F (120°C). Spray an 8-cup muffin pan with nonstick baking spray.

In a medium bowl, whisk together the flour and cocoa until they are thoroughly mixed.

In the bowl of a stand mixer with the paddle attachment, beat together the butter and powdered sugar. Scrape down the sides and bottom of the bowl and add the egg yolks, one at a time, beating after each addition. Scrape down the sides and bottom of the bowl and add the flour and cocoa powder on low speed. Mix until the dough comes together. Form the dough into a round ball.

Lightly flour a work surface and roll out the dough to a ¼-inch (6-mm) thickness. Using a 3¼-inch (8.2-cm) biscuit cutter, cut out six round pieces of dough. Gather the scraps and roll them out again to get two more rounds, for eight total. One cup at a time, use your fingers to press the dough into the muffin pan, so you have a crust of even thickness lining the bottom and sides of each cup (the dough should reach the rim of the cup). Set the muffin pan aside while you prepare the filling.

To make the cheesecake filling: In the bowl of a stand mixer with the paddle attachment, beat together the cream cheese and sugar until they're light and fluffy, about 3 minutes. Scrape down the sides and bottom of the bowl. Add the eggs, one at a time, scraping down the bowl after each addition. Add the melted chocolate, candy canes and salt. Beat on medium speed until everything is fully combined. Add the food coloring and mix until it's combined.

Scoop out 3 tablespoons (45 ml) of cheesecake batter into each cocoa crust. Bake the mini cheesecakes for 45 minutes. Remove them from the oven and cool them in the pan to room temperature.

To make the topping: In the bowl of a stand mixer with the whisk attachment, beat together the cream and sugar until stiff peaks form, about 3 minutes. Add the melted white chocolate.

Pipe or spoon the frosting onto the cheesecakes. Garnish with candy cane pieces. Place the cheesecakes in an airtight container and refrigerate for at least 4 hours. Serve chilled.

COCOA CRUST

1 cup (125 g) all-purpose flour

2 tbsp (11 g) unsweetened cocoa powder

6 tbsp (84 g) unsalted butter, cut into pieces

½ cup (60 g) powdered sugar

2 egg yolks

CHEESECAKE FILLING

8 oz (225 g) cream cheese, at room temperature

⅓ cup (66 g) granulated sugar

2 large eggs

¼ cup (42 g) white chocolate chips, melted

⅓ cup (56 g) crushed candy canes

⅛ tsp salt

2 drops pink food coloring

TOPPING

1 cup (240 ml) heavy cream

2 tbsp (30 g) granulated sugar

2 tbsp (30 ml) melted white chocolate

Candy cane pieces, for garnish

FRUITCAKE MONKEY BREAD

YIELD
Serves 6 to 8

People fear fruitcake. Perhaps it's the glowing candied fruit that sends them running. But I love it. I make a traditional fruitcake, and I make it as layer cake, as babka, as rolls and as crumb cake. But I had never made it as monkey bread. Boy, am I glad I did, as it is now the go-to for Christmas morning. It's fairly easy to throw together (way easier than cinnamon rolls) and it makes for a pretty presentation on your holiday breakfast table.

To make the monkey bread: Preheat the oven to 350°F (175°C). Generously spray a 12-cup (2.8-L) fluted tube pan with nonstick baking spray.

In a medium bowl, mix together ¾ cup (165 g) of the brown sugar and the cinnamon. Separate the biscuit dough into 16 biscuits and cut each into quarters. Roll each biscuit piece in the brown sugar mix, making sure the whole thing is coated.

Arrange one-third of the biscuit pieces in the prepared pan, and sprinkle one-third of the candied fruit pieces among the biscuit pieces. Add another one-third of the biscuit pieces and one-third of the candied fruits. Add the remaining biscuit pieces and the last of the candied fruits. Sprinkle any remaining brown sugar mix over the biscuits.

In a medium bowl, mix the remaining 1 cup (220 g) of brown sugar with the butter and rum. Pour everything over the biscuit pieces. Bake for 35 to 45 minutes, or until the top is golden brown and the bread is no longer doughy in the center. Loosen around the edges of the pan with a metal spatula. Cool the bread in the pan for 5 minutes. Invert it onto a serving plate, and reposition any biscuit pieces and caramel from the pan.

To make the glaze: In a small bowl, whisk together the orange juice, rum and powdered sugar until they're well mixed. Pour over the warm monkey bread and serve.

NOTES: Many people love nuts with their fruitcake. Feel free to add whatever nuts you like to the recipe when you add in the fruit pieces. If you do add nuts, I would add no more than ½ cup (about 55 g).

The recipe calls for rum in the bread, but the alcohol does bake out. It uses rum in the glaze as well, and that does not cook out. If you don't want the rum in the glaze simply use more orange juice.

MONKEY BREAD

1¾ cups (385 g) packed brown sugar, divided

1 tsp ground cinnamon

2 (8-count) packages Pillsbury Grands! Flaky Layers Original Biscuits

1½ cups (288 g) fruitcake mix candied fruits

¾ cup (170 g) unsalted butter

¼ cup (60 ml) rum

GLAZE

3 tbsp (45 ml) orange juice

2 tbsp (30 ml) rum

1 cup (120 g) powdered sugar

HOT CHOCOLATE CHEESECAKE CHEESEBALL

YIELD
Serves 6 to 8

In 2015 we had people over for my husband's birthday and watched the *Puppy Bowl* (there was football on, but hockey players don't watch football even for the commercials). I had the idea to make a sweet cheeseball and mix it with cake mix—it was for a birthday, after all. People could *not* get enough of it. It became one of the things I'm known for, and if I am going to any party people fully expect me to bring a dessert cheesecake cheeseball of some flavor. I have made many varieties over the years, but this one is extra special. This version is certainly right for the holidays. But since hot chocolate is enjoyed in all the cooler months, you can make it any time in the fall or winter.

1 lb (450 g) cream cheese, at room temperature

1 cup (227 g) unsalted butter, at room temperature

1½ cups (232 g) hot chocolate mix

1 cup (168 g) semisweet chocolate chips, melted and cooled

⅓ cup (35 g) unsweetened cocoa powder

1½ cups (180 g) powdered sugar

½ tsp vanilla extract

2 cups (80 g) Mallow Bits

½ cup (96 g) chocolate jimmies

Assorted cookies

Lay out a long piece of plastic wrap on the countertop.

In the bowl of a stand mixer with the paddle attachment, beat together the cream cheese and the butter until everything is fully incorporated. Add the hot chocolate mix, melted chocolate, cocoa powder, powdered sugar and vanilla. Beat until everything is fully incorporated.

Scoop the cream cheese mixture onto the plastic wrap. Do your best to form a ball, then wrap up the ball in the plastic wrap. Add an extra layer of plastic wrap to help it keep its shape. Freeze for about 2 hours.

Lay another long piece of plastic wrap on the countertop.

Take the ball out of the freezer and unwrap it. Mix up the Mallow Bits and chocolate jimmies in a shallow baking dish or a jelly roll pan (I find a plate is too small). Roll the ball in the mallow bits and jimmies, making sure you cover as much of it as you can. Your hands will get messy. Very messy.

Wrap the ball back up in the clean plastic wrap you laid out, and place it in the fridge. If you're not serving it that day, place it back in the freezer and take it out 1 hour before serving to come up to room temperature.

Serve with assorted cookies that you spread with the cheese.

NOTE: Mallow Bits and mini marshmallows are not the same thing. Mallow Bits are like the marshmallows you find in cereal or in the packaged cocoa that has marshmallows in the mix. You can usually find them at the grocery store, especially the larger chain stores.

STICKY BUN CINNAMON ROLL CHEESECAKE

YIELD
Serves 8 to 10

This is part sticky bun and part cheesecake. Or as I call it, Breakfast of Champions. Now before you scoff at the idea of eating this for breakfast, hear me out. People consider cinnamon rolls and sticky buns to be breakfast foods. Cheese danishes are a breakfast food that's basically cheesecake in a pastry. Therefore, sticky buns plus cheesecake is clearly a breakfast food.

Preheat the oven to 350°F (175°C). Spray a 9-inch (23-cm) springform pan with nonstick baking spray.

To make the sticky bun sauce: In a small heavy-bottomed saucepan, bring the brown sugar, butter and honey to a boil over medium-low heat, stirring frequently to dissolve the sugar. Add the pecans and whisk until they are fully incorporated. Set aside.

To make the sticky bun batter: In the bowl of a stand mixer with the paddle attachment, cream together the butter and sugar until they're light and fluffy, about 3 minutes. Add the egg, milk and vanilla and beat for another minute. Scrape down the sides and bottom of the bowl.

In a medium bowl, sift together the flour, baking powder and salt. Add the dry ingredients to the stand mixer bowl. Mix on low speed until all the ingredients are thoroughly combined. The dough will have more of a cookie texture than a cinnamon roll texture; that's because there is no yeast. Don't worry about it. Set aside.

To make the cheesecake filling: In another bowl of a stand mixer fitted with the paddle attachment, beat the cream cheese and sugar for 2 minutes on medium-high speed. Add the eggs one at a time, scraping down the bottom and sides of the bowl after each addition. Add the vanilla and flour and beat for another minute. Set aside.

(continued)

STICKY BUN SAUCE

1 cup (220 g) packed light brown sugar

½ cup (114 g) unsalted butter, cut into 4 pieces

¼ cup (60 ml) honey

1½ cups (164 g) whole shelled pecans

STICKY BUN BATTER

¼ cup (57 g) unsalted butter, at room temperature

⅔ cup (132 g) granulated sugar

1 large egg

½ cup (120 ml) whole milk

1 tbsp (15 ml) vanilla extract

2 cups (250 g) all-purpose flour

2 tsp (9 g) baking powder

½ tsp salt

CHEESECAKE FILLING

1 lb (450 g) cream cheese, at room temperature

1 cup (200 g) granulated sugar

3 large eggs

1 tbsp (15 ml) vanilla extract

2 tbsp (16 g) all-purpose flour

STICKY BUN CINNAMON ROLL CHEESECAKE (CONTINUED)

To make the cinnamon filling: In a small bowl, combine the melted butter, cinnamon, brown sugar and chopped pecans. Mix until they're thoroughly combined.

To assemble the cake: Spread half of the sticky bun batter in the bottom of the prepared pan. It will be sticky and thick, so spray your hands with nonstick baking spray and press down. It will be a thin layer, but trust me, it will rise during baking.

Pour half of the cheesecake filling on top of the sticky bun batter in the pan. Spread ½ cup (120 ml) of the sticky bun sauce on top of the cheesecake layer. (Place the rest of the sticky bun sauce in an airtight container and store it at room temperature until the cake is chilled.) Then spread the remaining cheesecake filling on top of that.

Drop spoonfuls of the cinnamon filling over the entire top of the cheesecake. Keep going until you have used it all up. Take the rest of the sticky bun batter and drop spoonfuls over the entire top of the cheesecake, leaving some spaces so you can see cheesecake.

When you're finished, use a knife to swirl the ingredients. This is hard to do, as the batter is pretty thick, so just do what you can. Swearing is allowed at this point.

Bake for about 50 to 55 minutes. The cake should be puffy and lightly browned. Let it cool in the pan for 20 minutes at room temperature, and then cover it with plastic wrap and refrigerate for 4 hours. Remove the cake from the fridge and let it warm up to room temperature. Top with the remaining sticky bun sauce that you put in the airtight container for later.

CINNAMON FILLING

⅓ cup (75 g) unsalted butter, melted

3 tbsp (24 g) ground cinnamon

1 cup (220 g) packed brown sugar

½ cup (55 g) chopped pecans

ORANGE-GLAZED GINGERBREAD BABKA

YIELD
Makes 2

I had never had a babka, and never really thought about them until I watched *Seinfeld* and the famous lesser babka episode, "The Dinner Party." Once I hunted one down and ate it, I was hooked. Babka is technically a yeasted cake, but almost everyone I know thinks of it as a bread. I make quite a few versions of it on my blog, all very untraditional, and have wanted to do a gingerbread version for a while now. This one does not disappoint, with a molasses gingerbread dough filled with orange marmalade and gingersnap cookies, all covered in an orange glaze.

To make the dough: Oil a large bowl, or spray it with nonstick baking spray. Set aside.

Add the yeast, warm water and brown sugar to the bowl of a stand mixer, and stir with a wooden spoon just until the sugar and yeast have dissolved. Let the mixture sit for 5 minutes for the yeast to activate.

With the dough hook attached to the stand mixer, add both flours, the salt and the granulated sugar to the bowl with the yeast. Mix on medium speed until everything is incorporated. Reduce the mixer speed to low and add the milk, eggs, molasses, vanilla and orange zest. Beat until the dough is shiny and elastic, 10 to 15 minutes. Add the butter one piece at a time until all the butter is fully incorporated, then beat the dough on low speed for about 5 minutes. The dough will look more like a batter than a yeasted dough. Remember that babka is a cake and not technically a bread, so you will not get a shiny round ball of dough. It will be sticky.

Transfer the dough to your prepared bowl, cover it with plastic wrap, and let the dough rise. When the dough has doubled in size, after about 2 hours, flour a cutting board and your hands. Push the dough down on the board to slightly deflate it. Cover the dough well with plastic wrap, keep it on the board and refrigerate the whole thing for 1 to 2 hours or overnight. I prefer overnight, but everyone has their own preference.

To make the filling: In a small bowl, mix together the crushed cookies, orange marmalade and butter, and set aside until you are ready to bake the babka.

To make the topping: In another small bowl, mix the flour, crushed cookies, brown sugar, salt and cinnamon. Add the butter pieces and, using your fingers, mix everything together until it's crumbly. Set aside until you are ready to bake the babka. (That's when you will need the melted butter.)

(continued)

DOUGH

2½ tsp (10 g) active dry yeast

1 tbsp (15 ml) water, warm (100–110°F [38–43°C])

1 tbsp (14 g) packed brown sugar

2 cups (250 g) all-purpose flour

¾ cup (90 g) cake flour

⅛ tsp salt

¼ cup (50 g) granulated sugar

½ cup (120 ml) whole milk, at room temperature

½ cup (120 ml) lightly beaten eggs (whole eggs or just yolks)

½ cup (120 ml) molasses

1 tsp vanilla extract

Zest of 1 orange

½ cup (114 g) unsalted butter, cut into pieces

FILLING

1½ cups (150 g) crushed gingersnap cookies

¾ cup (240 g) orange marmalade

¼ cup (60 ml) melted unsalted butter

TOPPING

5 tbsp (40 g) all-purpose flour

⅓ cup (35 g) crushed gingersnap cookies

3 tbsp (42 g) packed brown sugar

⅛ tsp salt

1 tsp ground cinnamon

3 tbsp (42 g) unsalted butter, cut into pieces, at room temperature

2 tbsp (30 ml) melted unsalted butter

ORANGE-GLAZED GINGERBREAD BABKA (CONTINUED)

To bake the babka: Line two 8½ x 4½-inch (22 x 11-cm) loaf pans with parchment paper. Do not let the paper stick up more than 1 inch (2.5 cm) above the top of the pans.

Remove the dough from the refrigerator and divide it in half. On a lightly floured surface, roll one piece of dough into an 8 x 12-inch (20 x 30-cm) rectangle. Using your fingers, crumble half of the filling evenly over the dough within ½ inch (13 mm) of the edges.

Beginning on the long side, roll the dough up tightly and fold in the ends. Hold one end of the babka in each hand and twist it lengthwise to create a spiral. Place the twisted babka in the prepared loaf pan, pressing the dough firmly into the pan. Brush the top of the babka with half the melted butter and sprinkle with half the topping.

Repeat with the second babka. Loosely cover both pans with plastic wrap. Let the loaves rise at room temperature until they reach the top of the pan or are about doubled in volume, about 2 hours.

Preheat the oven to 350°F (175°C).

Bake the babkas for about 45 minutes, or until a cake tester inserted in the center comes out clean. Cool the babkas in the pan for 15 minutes. Then remove them from the pan and let them cool at least 15 minutes more before icing them.

To make the icing: In a medium bowl, whisk together the sugar, marmalade and orange juice until they're smooth. Drizzle the icing over the two babkas. Let set at least 20 minutes before cutting them.

NOTE: All yeasted doughs take some time, but to me this one is well worth the effort.

ICING

1½ cups (180 g) powdered sugar

¼ cup (80 g) orange marmalade

1–2 tbsp (15–30 ml) orange juice

EGGNOG CRÈME CARAMEL

YIELD
Makes 6

I'll admit that I prefer my eggnog in a latte or a dessert rather than just drinking it straight. Then again, I prefer most things in dessert form. I'm not sure you can have a holiday chapter without an eggnog recipe. Crème caramel is one of those desserts that people rarely make at home—and they really should. It's part crème brûlée (minus the blowtorch) and part flan. All parts good. This recipe calls for making your own caramel, which does scare people. Be brave. You can do it.

CARAMEL

½ cup (100 g) granulated sugar

About 3 tbsp (45 ml) water

CUSTARD

2 cups (480 ml) heavy cream

1 cup (240 ml) eggnog (store-bought, not homemade)

3 egg yolks

2 large eggs

½ cup (100 g) granulated sugar

1 tsp freshly ground nutmeg

⅛ tsp salt

1 tsp vanilla extract

Preheat the oven to 325°F (160°C). Arrange six 6-ounce (177-ml) ramekins in a baking dish with high sides.

To make the caramel: Put the sugar in a small, clean saucepan. Carefully add just enough water to dissolve the sugar, stirring as you add the water. When the sugar is dissolved, set the pot over high heat. After a few minutes, the mixture will come to a full boil. Several minutes later the sugar will start to color. Swirl the pan around to even out the caramelization, or it will color in just one spot and eventually burn. Once the sugar has started to caramelize, watch it carefully. (Seriously, don't be doing anything else but staring at the pan.) It takes just seconds for caramel to go from great to burned.

When the caramel is an even dark brown (which can take anywhere from 8 to 10 minutes), carefully pour it into the ramekins. The caramel will be super hot, so please be careful. Divide it evenly so that each ramekin is lined with a thin layer of dark brown caramel. Let it cool so the caramel can set while you make the custard.

To make the custard: In a medium saucepan, heat the cream and eggnog over medium heat until they're scalded. You'll see small bubbles on the sides of the pan. (Feel free to sing "Tiny Bubbles" at this time. . . . I always do.)

Put the egg yolks and eggs in a medium bowl and slowly whisk in the sugar until it is fully combined. Then whisk ¼ cup (60 ml) of the hot cream and eggnog into the sugar and yolk mixture. Continue to do this ¼ cup (60 ml) at a time until all the cream and eggnog has been whisked in.

Strain the mixture through a fine sieve into a pitcher or measuring cup, in case any egg cooked a little. Whisk in the nutmeg, salt and vanilla.

(continued)

To finish the crème caramels: Pour the custard mix evenly into the caramel-lined ramekins. Put the baking dish with the ramekins in the oven. Fill the dish with enough hot water to come halfway up the sides of the ramekins, then cover the whole dish with aluminum foil. Bake until the custard is just set, 25 to 50 minutes. That seems like a really wide range, but how your ramekin is shaped (thickness and depth) will affect how long it takes to bake.

Carefully remove the baking dish from the oven and let the ramekins cool in the water bath. When they're cool, remove the foil and take them out of the pan. Cover each one with plastic wrap and refrigerate at least 2 hours or up to 2 days.

To serve, run a thin knife around the edge of the custard and invert it onto a dessert plate. Scrape any caramel still in the ramekin onto the custard.

NOTES: When you're making the custard, do not try to add the hot liquid all at once. Slow and steady tempers the eggs so they do not turn the mixture into scrambled eggs.

Be sure to use store-bought eggnog and not homemade. Homemade tends to have more eggs and it makes the custard far too eggy.

ACKNOWLEDGMENTS

To my mom, Jane, who never crushed my creativity growing up even though you silently sat in the kitchen while your eye twitched watching me make a giant mess. You don't own a computer and never go on the Internet so I had to break down and write a book for you. And not the scandalous tell-all book I threatened to write about you when I was a moody teenager. Thank you for spending hours on the phone with me discussing recipes and talking about people in your small town that I have no idea who they are but I pretend I do.

To my husband, Jason, who got stuck with months and months of eating way too many desserts and not enough real food. Who puts up with my bleeding heart of needing to save special needs spaniels by also having a bleeding heart that agrees we need to rescue spaniels. Who eats anything I put in front of him with an adventurous spirit. Thanks for always making me smile when I'm having a bad day, giving me unwavering support and love and for passing the puck to me sometimes when we play hockey.

To my dad, Ed, who survived my cocktail-making years. The man I tried to learn the bagpipes for even though you woke me up as a teenager on the weekends by blaring "Scotland the Brave" at decibels no one should be subjected to. Thank you for all your support over the years and for letting me be your favorite daughter.

To my blog readers, especially the ones who have been there since the beginning, I really do wish I could give you a badge or something for surviving all these years. Thank you for being my muses, my friends, my supporters and the people who write me e-mails asking for a refund on muffins they made.

To Kita, my kick-ass food blogger buddy who is somehow my polar opposite and kindred spirit all the same. You know this book would not exist without you. For real.

To Laurie, the woman I made my matron of honor, even though I had never physically met her in person until the wedding. That is the power of the Internet, people. Thank you for always having my back even when I don't get to talk to you for months.

To Justin, who keeps the blog alive and running and gets stuck being the IT guy. Thank you for all your support over the years.

To Jill O'Connor, my cookbook author crush, who has encouraged me over and over and over again through the years to write a book of my own. Thank you for letting me know I could do it.

To my editor, Marissa Giambelluca, and the whole staff over at Page Street Publishing who helped make this book possible. Thank you for thinking that a girl who wanted a chapter in her book to be called "Cereal Killers" sounded like a good idea. Thank you for getting me and my quirkiness and allowing it to come to print.

To Julie, our pet photographer, who I somehow convinced to do my headshot for the book.

To my Black Sheep hockey team, who selflessly (cough, cough) eats my baked goods week after week to provide me with feedback.

To my spaniel peeps: To Marie who loves to try all of my recipes. To Kari who sends the best care packages that always come at the right time to cheer me up. To Karen who lets me bring all my dogs and sit around in pajamas at her house and is always so supportive. And to all of the Cavalier Instagram community who have given my whole family such love and support.

ABOUT THE AUTHOR

PEABODY JOHANSON is a former math and physical science teacher, current third place Trophy Wife and full-time recipe developer and blogger. Self-proclaimed homebody. Baking fanatic. Inept housekeeper. Kitchen mess maker. British Bake-Off junkie. Full-time vegetarian, part-time lush. Avid reader, Netflix binger. Sweatpants connoisseur.

Peabody started blogging before food blogging was a thing, in 2005. Back then her blog was called Culinary Concoctions by Peabody. But since that was a mouthful, she changed it to better represent her, renaming it Sweet ReciPEAS, with a play on words of her name.

Peabody comes from the food blogging days when people started food blogs not as a business but as a way to express their creativity and to connect with others who also shared a passion for baking.

When she's not baking in her tiny kitchen, Peabody runs a men's league ice hockey team, where she plays defense with her husband, Jason. She also rescues special needs and senior Cavalier King Charles Spaniels as well as English Toy Spaniels. Specializing in adopting spaniels with mitral valve disease and congestive heart failure, her work with them is both rewarding and heartbreaking.

INDEX